SHOPPING FOR A BETTER WORLD

A Quick and Easy Guide to
Socially Responsible
Supermarket Shopping

by
Ben Corson,
Alice Tepper Marlin,
Jonathan Schorsch,
Anitra Swaminathan,
and Rosalyn Will

CEP
COUNCIL ON
ECONOMIC
PRIORITIES

Council on Economic Priorities

MADE FROM RECYCLED PAPER

Printed on 100% recycled paper

The Council on Economic Priorities wishes to thank especially The Cook Brothers Educational Fund for its vision and generosity in making this guide possible. Our deep appreciation also to Marion Weber, The Mary Reynolds Babcock Foundation, The Wilson Foundation and The Horncrest Foundation for their generous support of this project; to Lyn Severance and Sarah Lee Terrat of Ben & Jerry's Homemade for cover design and graphics; to the Community Typesetter, Inc., for design and quality typesetting; to the interns who helped research the guide: Ivanya Alpert, Ji-Young Chung, Margaret LaForce, David Mitchell, and Stacey Steinmetz, some of whom were sponsored by The Henry and Edith Everett Public Service Intern Program; and last but not least to all the CEP staff who pitched in.

Copyright © 1989 by the Council on Economic Priorities

ISBN# 0-87871-058-2

Council on Economic Priorities
30 Irving Place, New York, NY 10003
212-420-1133

Second Edition, Second Printing

G90-2

TABLE OF CONTENTS

"I use this handy guide every time I shop. It gives me the substance — not the slogans — I need to buy products that really do contribute to a safer, cleaner world."
                              — Pauline Quan, Chicago, IL

"The 20-year-old Council on Economic Priorities' new booklet Shopping For A Better World: A Quick and Easy Guide to Socially Responsible Supermarket Shopping *is a moral report card on 138 parent companies and the 1,300 products they make. Consumers are encouraged to let their consciences do the walking in 10 areas . . ."*
                              — Newsweek

Interviewing Alice Tepper Marlin on NBC's Today Show on December 27th, host Bryant Gumbel declared, "I like this guide!," and told people how to order it.
                              — Bryant Gumbel, NBC's Today Show

"Easy to use . . . Good news for those who want to turn their shopping carts into vehicles for social change."
                              — New Age Journal

"Shopping For a Better World makes consumers more aware of the companies behind the products they buy: the real companies, not the elves making cookies in hollow trees and svelte models hawking products so light and low in everything you'd think you were buying nothing but deliciously flavored air."
                              — Dallas Observer

"People are starting to demand that corporations live up to the expectations that we have of them as citizens," says Alice Tepper Marlin, executive director of the Manhattan-based Council on Economic Priorities. While most Americans still feel confident about the economy and business in general, consumers have become increasingly aggressive in taking corporations to task for misbehavior and irresponsibility."
— **Time Magazine**

" 'This type of report has an impact when the consumer is going down the aisle,' said Campbell Soup Company spokesman David Hackney."
— **Philiidelphia Inquirer**

"Shopping For a Better World *is an easy, practical way for all of us to support companies that recycle waste, make biodegradable products and are environmentally responsible. By using this guide we can all contribute to a cleaner, greener world."*
— **Mike McCloskey, Chairman, Sierra Club**
Washington, DC

" 'Corporate citizen' is often heard as a phrase, but the Council on Economic Priorities takes it to heart. By monitoring and encouraging corporations to be good citizens, CEP is changing the workplace, the marketplace and the world."
— **Gloria Steinem**

WHAT IS SHOPPING FOR A BETTER WORLD?

As you flip through the pages of **SHOPPING FOR A BETTER WORLD**, you will notice many familiar names. You will see your favorite brand of cereal, your gas station, the all-natural toothpaste made by the small health food company you just read about in the paper, and the supermarket you visit at least once a week to do your shopping. These are companies and products you are exposed to every day. Yet how much do you really know about the companies you are supporting with your hard-earned dollars? Some companies continue to sell strategic products to the South African military and police or spew toxic fumes into the atmosphere, further damaging our dangerously fragile ecosystem. Others donate large portions of their profits to charity, revitalize their local communities, and value the expertise of women and people of color in their highest levels of management. **SHOPPING FOR A BETTER WORLD** provides you with the information necessary to tell one kind of product from another, so you can select products from companies whose policies and practices you support.

Of course, no one but you can decide which products to buy for yourself and your family. Quality, safety, nutrition, and price may top your list of priorities. If a certain brand is on sale, or is the only peanut butter your child will eat, chances are that's what you'll put in your shopping cart. But often, in a sea of competing detergents or canned peas, differences are minimal. Product differentiations created by advertising can be misleading or just plain trivial.

Using the information gathered here you can feel good about your purchases and truly shop for a better world. Today's corporations wield enormous power and influence. With minimal effort and expense this power could be used for the benefit of both the company and the community.

You may feel powerless to influence corporate practices. **SHOPPING FOR A BETTER WORLD** helps empower you by providing information which you would have a hard time finding on your own. It gives you the opportunity to influence corporate policy by providing the addresses, phone numbers, and names of chief executive officers for all the companies in this guide (see page 242). You can have an enormous impact upon a company by switching brands and telling the Chief Executive Officer why. Ultimately, companies want your business and the sensible ones will change their ways if enough people let them know they care.

You can also apply our rating system to your own place of work, whether you are a production line worker or the president of the company. To rate your workplace, use the worksheet provided at the end of the rating charts (page 233).

HOW TO USE THIS GUIDE

The ratings in **SHOPPING FOR A BETTER WORLD** are divided into two main sections. The first section alphabetically lists all the companies that appear in the guide. Small companies (less than 100 employees) are listed separately, as are supermarkets and oil companies. The second section is arranged alphabetically by product category (e.g. Baby Food or Bread). Within each product category, brand names are arranged alphabetically.

As you shop, search for either the brand name or the company name of the product you are interested in knowing more about. Each entry is followed by 13 columns. The first contains an abbreviation for the company that makes the product (see abbreviation index on page 274). The information in the next 12 columns all applies to that specific company. **SHOPPING FOR A BETTER WORLD** rates companies according to their performance in the following issue areas: Charitable Giving, Women's Advancement, Advancement of People of Color, Military Contracts, Animal Testing, Disclosure of Information, Community Outreach, Nuclear Power, South Africa, Environment, and Family Benefits.

Most of these issues are rated using the symbols ✔, ⩗, or ✘ A ✔ indicates outstanding performance, ⩗ indicates moderate or mixed performance, and ✘ indicates poor performance. A few of the issues are rated on a Yes/No scale. "Yes" indicates some involvement and "No" indicates no involvement. See the rating key on page 10 for more information. A "?"

means that despite much research, we could not find sufficient information to make a rating. All products made by any one company and its subsidiaries will have the same rating.

Please see the Rating Key preceding the charts (page 10) for detailed explanations of each rating.

Small companies, almost all with a staff of fewer than 100 people and a few of which employ less than 10 people, are indicated with a number sign (#) after their name.

The final column, labelled "ALERT" contains important information about the company that could not be shown by the ratings alone. An ALERT glossary on page 236 explains each phrase in detail.

SHOPPING FOR A HEALTHIER LIFE

Knowledgeable shoppers everywhere are waking up. You're reading labels instead of just listening to commercials. You're paying more attention to the nutrients inside the package, and less to the catchy offers on the side of the box.

Chances are you have a written grocery list in your hand, and another far more important one in your head . . .

REDUCE PURCHASE OF FOOD CONTAINING:

- Sodium — fresh foods contain enough salt.

- Fat, cholesterol — cut down on animal fat; use fish and poultry rather than pork and beef, especially fatty cuts; avoid egg yolks; cook by steaming; choose olive or sunflower oil; avoid fried foods.

- Sugar and alchohol — empty calories, no nutrition.

- Additives — especially avoid nitrite and artificial coloring.

INCREASE PURCHASE OF FOOD CONTAINING:

- Fiber — more fruit, vegetables, whole grains, bran, and nuts.

- Foods grown organically

But it doesn't stop there. You're discovering that highly processed foods not only rob your family of good nutrition, but also are wasteful to produce. *You* can choose alternatives. **Fresh foods rich in fiber,** for example, not only help guard against digestive diseases like colon cancer, but also generate less waste and use less energy in the production process. For the best nutrition, eat locally grown vegetables and fruit raw. Alternatively, steam or poach them. Avoid "fast food" restaurants. For really terrific nutrition and environmental citizenship, grow your own vegetables, fruits and nuts organically with your own compost.

When it comes to shopping, in fact, we imagine you've become a bit of an expert on the products you buy every day. Now with **SHOPPING FOR A BETTER WORLD**, you can learn more about the companies that make them.

COUNCIL ON ECONOMIC PRIORITIES

In 1969, when CEP was founded, there was little consensus that corporations have a responsibility to address such social issues as the environment, charitable giving, and the handicapped.

Today, twenty years later, that climate has changed and the Council on Economic Priorities has helped change it.

CEP has painstakingly gathered and documented facts in more than 1,000 publications - major studies, reports, and newsletters - on subjects as diverse as the B-1 bomber, child care, air pollution, occupational safety, and the politics of defense contracting.

Some of our major publications are: *Rating America's Corporate Conscience* (Addison Wesley, 1987), which assesses the social records of 130 U.S. companies and *Star Wars: the Economic fallout* (Ballinger/Harper & Row, 1988), which details the economic consequences of SDI spending estimated to cost as much as $1 trillion.

In mid 1990, CEP's new book, *Investing in America's Corporate Conscience*, will be published by Prentice Hall. That book will include a history of the ethical investing movement, profiles of major ethical funds and ratings of 100 publicly held companies.

CEP's goal is to inform and educate the American public and provide incentives for corporations to be good corporate citizens by being responsive to the social concerns of investors and consumers.

CEP also produces the annual America's Corporate Conscience Awards ceremony. Chaired by CEO's of companies which are past winners, the gala event honors corporations for outstanding achievements in a particular area and also gives "dishonorable mention" to corporations which have disregarded the public good.

- CEP is an independent, non-profit public interest research organization which is supported by a nationwide membership as well as by individual and foundation grants.

- All CEP members receive a free copy of the annually updated **SHOPPING FOR A BETTER WORLD** immediately upon its release. To join, simply send in the order form in the back of this book.

SHOPPING FOR A BETTER WORLD — THE IMPACT

More than 600,000 copies of **SHOPPING FOR A BETTER WORLD** have been sold and they have already affected decision making.

In a CEP poll we conducted of 968 buyers of the Guide an impressive 78% of the respondents said they had "switched brands" because of **SHOPPING FOR A BETTER WORLD** ratings. 98% told us that all 10 issues were important to them. 64% referred to the **SHOPPING FOR A BETTER WORLD** ratings whenever they shopped, and 97% considered the environment their top or near top priority.

People all across the country tell us what they think (see page 271). Some write to corporations, too, and send us copies of their letters.

And the companies are responding!

- Campbell Soup Company tells us **SHOPPING FOR A BETTER WORLD** and its ratings are referred to by participants in numerous focus groups around the country.

- Borden executives requested a meeting with CEP staff to ask what Borden needs to do to get a top rating in every category. After the meeting, they planned to recommend specific improvements and new programs to their chief executive officer.

- Unilever, Borden, Hormel and others which absolutely refused to provide information last year were fully cooperative this year.

- Ben & Jerry's Homemade sent a letter to all of their suppliers to let them know that whenever more than one supplier could meet Ben & Jerry's standards for quality and reliability, B & J's would select the supplier with the better social performance. The letter told suppliers about **SHOPPING FOR A BETTER WORLD**. A detailed questionnaire was enclosed based on the one we used at CEP for our research and asked each recipient to fill out and return the form.

RATING KEY

In general, a ✔ rating indicates outstanding performance in the issue area as defined by the rating key. A ⦸ means moderate performance or mixed record, and an ✘ indicates basically poor performance or little evidence of a good record. For all categories, a rating of "?" means insufficient information on which to base a rating. Small companies, whose entire staff may number between three and one hundred persons, are marked with a number sign (#) on the rating sheet.

 GIVING TO CHARITY:

Total worldwide *cash* donations (including direct corporate giving, foundation giving, and matching gifts) for the most recent year is figured as a percentage of the average of three previous years' pre-tax worldwide earnings.

✔+ — 2% or more of net pre-tax earnings given to charity.

✔ — Over 1%.

⦸ — Over 0.6%, up to 1%.

✘ — 0.6% or less.

 WOMEN'S ADVANCEMENT:

CEP has looked at representation of women on a company's Board of Directors as well as among the company's top officers (Vice-Presidential level or higher at corporate HQ or President/CEO of a subsidiary or division). This is only one indication of a company's responsiveness to its women employees. See the Family Benefits category for other information on how companies are responding to the changing workforce.

✔ — At least two women on the Board of Directors and one among top officers (or vice versa).

✅ — At least one woman on the Board or among top officers.

✘ — No women on the Board or among top officers.

Where information was available, these ratings have been adjusted up or down according to Equal Employment Opportunity Commission reports of percentage of women among Officials and Managers, company size and industry to which it belongs, and purchasing from women-owned firms.

 # ADVANCEMENT OF PEOPLE OF COLOR:

CEP has looked at representation of people of color on a company's Board of Directors as well as among the company's top officers (Vice-Presidential level or higher at corporate HQ or President/CEO of a subsidiary or division). This is only one indication of a company's responsiveness to employees who are people of color.

✔ — At least two people of color on the Board of Directors and one among top officers (or vice versa).

✅ — At least one person of color on the Board or among top officers.

✘ — No people of color on the Board or among top officers.

Where information was available, these ratings have been adjusted up or down according to Equal Employment Opportunity Commission reports of percentage of people of color among Officials and Managers, company size and type of industry, purchasing from minority-owned firms, and banking with minority-owned banks.

MILITARY CONTRACTS:

No — Company has no nuclear weapons-related contracts over $1 million, and is not on the 1988 Department of Defense Top 100 list for either weapons manufacture or supply of fuel.

Yes — Company appears as a weapons maker or fuel supplier in 1988 Department of Defense Top 100 list of parent companies receiving largest dollar volume of prime contract awards and/or is listed among top 100 prime contractors for Research, Development, Test and Evaluation work.

Yes∗ — Company has nuclear weapons-related contract(s) over $1 million.

 ANIMAL TESTING:

Clear guidelines for rating companies on animal testing are difficult to achieve for a variety of reasons: 1) While some testing may be performed for a lipstick or cleanser, other tests are used to further research on drugs for battling cancer or AIDS; 2) Some companies manufacture both medical products and consumer products and may test animals for both; and 3) Companies may sell off or acquire a subsidiary that uses animal testing, causing fluctuations difficult to quantify.

CEP has tried, therefore, to present a straightforward assessment of whether a company tests or not, and if so, the extent to which it seeks to reduce numbers of animals used and explores non-animal alternatives.

✔ — No animal testing.
✔∗ — Company tests on animals but has reduced the number used in testing by 40% or more over the last five years and/or has given $250,000 or more to alternative research through in-house or independent labs.

✘ — Company tests on animals; no quantitative report of reductions or major contributions to alternative research.

A ◯ following any rating indicates that the company manufactures surgical/medical supplies and/or prescription drugs.

 ## DISCLOSURE OF INFORMATION:

✔ — Company provided substantial and substantive materials on its social programs and policies either by completing CEP's questionnaire or providing comparable information in printed matter or phone interviews.
✔ — Company provided some specific information either by partially completing CEP's questionnaire or providing comparable information in printed matter or phone interviews. Certain key questions were left unanswered.
✘ — Company provided only the most basic information: an annual report, proxy statement and 10K, or less; or, if additional information were provided, it was not detailed enough to give any real indication of the company's performance.

 ## COMMUNITY OUTREACH:

✔ — Strong programs promoting education, housing and/or volunteerism; little or no evidence of major labor disputes or litigation.
✔ — Moderate community programs *or* mixed record: some good initiatives but some evidence of major litigation or labor disputes.
✘ — Little or no evidence of programs designed to benefit community, and/or record shows major lawsuits or labor disputes.

NUCLEAR POWER:

No — Company has no involvement with nuclear power.

Yes — Company supplies one or more of the following to the nuclear power industry: construction, production equipment, fuel or consulting.

 ## SOUTH AFRICA:

No — No involvement in South Africa.
Yes — Licensing, distribution, and/or franchising agreements: non-strategic.
Yes● — Investment: non-strategic.
Yes* — Investment, licensing, distribution, and/or franchising agreements: strategic.
Yes† — Company has a foreign-based parent with investment, licensing, distribution, and/or franchising agreements in South Africa.

Note: All but 3 companies in **SHOPPING FOR A BETTER WORLD** with investment in South Africa have signed the Statement of Principles and have received the top rating, I, (making good progress) in the most recent year. Two exceptions are Revlon and Caltex (a joint venture in which Chevron and Texaco each have a 50% interest). Both these companies have received a IIA rating — making progress based on full reporting. One company, Kimberly-Clark, is a non-signatory.

Definition of Strategic: A company is considered strategic either by the nature of its product (e.g. oil for sale to The South African military or police) or by the size of its operations — the amount of assets or number of employees in South Africa.

ENVIRONMENT: Large companies

✔ — Positive programs, such as the use and encouragement of: recycling, alternative energy sources, waste reduction, etc. A record relatively clear of major regulatory violations.

◌ — A mixed record: some positive programs such as use and encouragement of recycling, alternative energy sources, waste reduction, etc. Problems such as accidents, regulatory infractions, fines, complaints, etc.

✘ — Company has a poor public record of significant violations, major accidents and/or history of lobbying against sound environmental policies.

 ENVIRONMENT: Small companies

✔ — Makes strong effort to: 1) use biodegradable and/or recyclable materials in packaging products; 2) dispose of waste from manufacturing process in an environmentally sound way; and 3) use only natural ingredients and organic growing techniques for food.

◌ — Moderate effort to achieve above.

✘ — Little or no effort to achieve above.

 FAMILY BENEFITS:

CEP has rated companies according to how many of the following family benefits they had in at least one location or division.

Parental Leave: Paid disability period for maternity (usually 6-8 weeks).

Child and/or Dependent Care Assistance: Reimbursement, Referral, On-site day care.

Flextime: An arrangement whereby an employee may arrive and leave earlier, while working certain core hours and maintaining regular number of hours in workday; special summer hours were taken into account.

Jobsharing: Two employees share one job, working morning or afternoon to suit needs.

Flexible Benefits: May include comprehensive "cafeteria" plans or more limited spending accounts funded by employee salary reductions.

✔ — 4 or 5 of the benefits.
✓ — 3 of the benefits.
✗ — 0, 1, or 2 of the benefits.

Rating improves if —

1) Parental leave for childbirth, paid or unpaid, may be extended beyond eight-week disability period.

2) Paid or unpaid leave is available for adoption, acquiring of foster child, or care of sick family member.

If benefits were in experimental stage or in process of being implemented, CEP counted it as a "yes." A benefit still in research stage was counted as a "no." The size of the company and type of industry were also considered. this is the first time CEP has included a family benefits category. A benefit granted through "departmental discretion" or on a "case-by-case" basis has been counted as a "yes." This may change in future editions of **SHOPPING FOR A BETTER WORLD**, since only a company-wide written policy can eliminate the possibility of discrimination.

ALERT:

Highlights important information that cannot be indicated by the ratings alone. A glossary at the back of the guide explains the ALERTs in more detail (see page 236 for the glossary).

SHOPPING FOR GENEROUS CHARITABLE GIVING

Corporate donations have come a long way since one major manufacturer supplied soap and candles to the town hospital.

In recent years, many corporations have helped to alleviate problems caused by deep cuts in federal funding for housing, education, and child care. They have contributed money and products to food banks such as Second Harvest, instituted job-training programs for disadvantaged youths, and set up partnerships with local governments to revitalize communities. Some have joined the flagship 2% and 5% clubs, whose members pledge those portions of their pre-tax income to charitable causes. Newman's Own gives 100% of profits; Tom's of Maine and Ben and Jerry's Homemade give 7.5%.

At one time companies channelled their charitable dollars to a wide range of causes, giving many small grants to groups with such diverse concerns as the arts and policy analysis. Now more companies are concentrating on one or two causes.

The cause attracting the most attention is education. In the past, contributions went to research universities and colleges. The newest recipients of corporate gifts are secondary and elementary schools. Corporations see the graduates of today's schools and realize that a growing number are unprepared even for the most basic entry-level tasks. Thus, by helping the schools financially they are combining self-interest with philanthropy. Everybody comes out a winner.

Although most corporate giving is done through company foundations and direct corporate giving, many companies have programs which match employee gifts to non-profit organizations. A few companies give a generous $3 for every $1 an employee donates. Others give grants to groups for whom their employees volunteer.

Another method of giving which is of increasing interest to today's profit-minded CEOs is cause-related marketing, in which companies promise to donate a certain amount of the purchase price of their product to charity. The more of their product they sell, the more money they give away. Still other companies make substantial in-kind gifts. Neither cause-related marketing proceeds nor in-kind donation are included in our charity ratings, which are calculated as a percentage of worldwide pre-tax earnings.

Giving as a percentage of pre-tax net income rose steadily for 16 years until 1985 when it reached its peak of almost 2%. Since then, corporate generosity has declined: 1.9% in 1986 and 1.7% in 1987. Corporate giving in 1988 reached the lowest percentage in six years, 1.6%. These figures include in-kind donations and are figured as a percentage of domestic pre-tax earnings. Despite this gloomy trend you can help shape the future of charitable giving:

- "Give Five." Contribute 5% of your income to charity. The current U.S. average for individuals is 2.4%.
- Support companies that are members of 2% or 5% clubs. Companies are allowed to give up to 10% of pre-tax income.
- Ask your employer to match your gifts generously and to donate money to the organizations where you volunteer.
- Help raise money for your favorite causes.
- Support companies rated ✔+ or ✔.

SHOPPING FOR
EQUAL OPPORTUNITY

The U.S. Department of Labor estimates that by the 1990's over three-fourths of all new entrants into the U.S. workforce will be people of color or women. This revealing statistic should send a clear message to the corporations of America: the traditional barriers blocking advancement for people of color and women must be toppled.

One needs to look no further than a daily newspaper to find evidence that these barriers exist today:

— 1987 Bureau of Labor statistics show
  Afro-Americans earned $306 per week
  Hispanics earned $316 per week
  White Americans earned $391 per week

— Women working full-time earn 65¢ for every $1.00 a man earns, according to the Census Bureau.

— Many boards of directors of major companies still do not have even one female participant; a greater number lack people of color.

Some companies already have systems in place to eliminate barriers to the advancement of qualified women and people of color. They have Upward Mobility Committees, mentoring programs, advertising in women's and minorities' publications, and regularly review their personnel managers' records of hiring women and minorities.

There has been some positive change over the years, in part due to programs like these. The total number of women directors of Fortune 1000 companies in 1988 was 571, up from 46 in 1969. Still, more than 400 Fortune 1000 companies do not have a single woman on their boards. People of color have even less representation.

Even companies located in areas where people of color make up only a small portion of the population or companies in industries where the pool of qualified women applicants is limited can have an impact. By seeking out businesses owned by people of color or women as suppliers, companies provide invaluable experience and revenues. Other companies choose to keep their money in banks owned by people of color or women, or in "greenlining" banks like South Shore Bank in Chicago. The banks, in turn, are apt to lend the money to companies run by women and people of color, doubling the effectiveness of the initial deposit.

The growth of minority purchasing and banking programs has been encouraging. In 1972, the purchasing programs reported $86 million in business. By 1987 that figure had reached $10.5 **billion**. Approximately 74 of the Fortune 500 companies were using minority banking programs in 1988, an impressive leap from the 15 companies in 1984.

There is still a long way to go, but you can help:
- Encourage your place of work to seek out banks and suppliers owned by women and people of color.
- Let your elected representatives know you support enforcement of Equal Employment Opportunity laws.
- Be color-blind yourself. Give women and people of color a fair break.
- Teach your children to do the same.
- Join organizations that speak out for a fair break for women and people of color.
- Select products made by companies rated ✔ in women's advancement and advancement of people of color.

SHOPPING FOR REAL NATIONAL SECURITY

Most of the companies in **SHOPPING FOR A BETTER WORLD** sell consumer products to the Department of Defense. Few are significantly involved in weapons production or fuel supply as indicated by their presence among top 100 DoD contractors or by manufacturing weapons systems or their components.

The need to reduce the national deficit, concern about waste and mismanagement of defense programs, and renewed cooperative efforts at arms control with the Soviet Union have brought the defense budget under increasing Congressional scrutiny. Bipartisan consensus is building for a leaner defense budget. Most American households paid $21,000 each for their share of Reagan's defense budget and now feel that increases in military expenditures can no longer be justified. According to a March 1988 poll conducted by Daniel Yankelovich, *Americans Talk Security*, 72 percent of those polled feel we should be spending more on "economic programs to create jobs and economic growth" while only 14 percent say we should be spending more on "military spending and national security."

By freezing the FY 1990 defense budget, the Bush Administration signalled the end of the Reagan $2 trillion military buildup. The budget had jumped from $217 billion to $299 billion in just 8 years. The $305 billion 1990 budget, by contrast, is nearly 12 percent lower in real terms than it was in 1985 — the peak of the buildup. Defense programs such as the Midgetman, SDI, MX, Stealth bomber, F-14 navy fighter, V-22 helicopter, and F-15 air force fighter, among others, are already being targetted by the budget axe. But they are only the tip of the iceberg. What is needed is a fundamental overhaul of defense policy.

Too often, porkbarrel politics and military contractor lobbying get in the way of real national security. Regions whose economies have traditionally been dependent on defense contracting are hard put to support defense cutbacks because of the jobs and income generated by military work. For example, the 25 leading recipients of political action committee contributions from top SDI contractors voted against lowering the SDI budget 83 percent of the time in five key votes between 1984 and 1986.

If we are to make any progress on redefining our national security, clearly the debate should focus on the value of the program for the nation's defense and not merely on its costs. In its new project, *Strategies for a Productive America*, CEP will examine the potential impact of defense cutbacks on regions throughout the country and the measures that might be taken to make a smooth transition to a less defense-dependent economy.

If our defense budget is restored to a more rational balance, with a treaty cutting strategic nuclear weapons by 50 percent, a nuclear test ban, a chemical weapons ban, and a solid conventional arms treaty in place, CEP will remove this category from our rating system. CEP and two prominent Soviet institutes will jointly examine the economic benefits these arms control agreements may bring to both our economies.

As an individual, you can make a difference:

- Join an organization that speaks out and organizes for real national security.
- Let your Representative know that progress should quickly be made towards agreements to reduce strategic nuclear and conventional weapons.
- If you agree with Pentagon lobbyists that we need more technologically advanced weapons, select products made by companies rated "Yes" or "Yes*."
- If you are convinced that mutual security offers more real national security, select products made by companies rated "No."

SHOPPING TO END ANIMAL TESTING

During the last decade, the complex issue of using animals in product safety testing, particularly for cosmetics, has become more visible and controversial. Much of the debate centers on whether the federal Food and Drug Administration (FDA) requires that animal tests be performed before a new cosmetic can be put on the market. Dr. Richard Bradberry, FDA's Director of Animal Care and Use, stated in April, 1989: "Current laws administered by the FDA do not require the use of animal testing for cosmetics. [However], the FDA strongly urges cosmetic manufacturers to conduct whatever toxicological or other tests are appropriate to substantiate the safety of the cosmetics . . . As it stands now, many years of further research and broad advances on all fronts of toxicological, medical and related scientific disciplines will be required to replace animal testing methods with non-animal techniques. Various scientific efforts are under way to reach this goal. Let us hope the time will come when the safety of regulated products can be predicted without the need for animal testing."

Most smaller companies use only ingredients that are already acceptable through previous testing ("generally recognized as safe"). Large companies, under competitive pressure to bring a constant stream of new products to market, are more likely to develop formulas with hitherto untried ingredients.

A public increasingly concerned with the massive suffering of animals has insisted, however, that their use for cosmetic and other product testing be reduced, and alternative methods to ensure human safety be developed. In 1989, after years of research, three giant U.S. cosmetic companies announced cessation of all animal testing. They will use non-animal test alternatives and data banks of previously-tested ingredients and formulations to ensure the safety of future products. Other sectors of the corporate community have launched programs — from special in-house committees to industry-wide symposia — to promote non-animal alternatives. These new methods may well be faster, cheaper, and more reliable. Recent efforts have substantially reduced the LD50 (which determines the toxicity level of a substance required to kill 50 percent of animals in a test group), the Draize rabbit eye, and other tests.

Another dramatic example of modern technology phasing animals out of the laboratory is the National Cancer Institute (NCI)'s anti-tumor drug discovery program. Driven by the need to gain better scientific results, the NCI has (since 1986) reduced its use of animals from six million to less than 300,000 a year. The Institute reports that the program (using human tumor cell lines) promises to be more dependable and cost-effective, as well.

Still, much remains to be done, particularly to reduce the pain and suffering of animals being tested. While many consumer and household product companies have tried to reduce the number of animals used and/or joined the search for alternative test methods, they account for less than one percent of the estimated 17 to 70 million lab animals used every year. Treatment of farm animals is also an issue of concern for many animal lovers, but at this point in time, CEP does not have enough information to rate company performance.

For the chronically ill, who in the past have depended on research performed primarily on animals for cure or relief, efforts to completely eliminate such research are life-threatening. Over 2,000 victims of diseases such as AIDS, heart disease and muscular dystrophy have formed IIFAR (Incurably Ill for Animal Research) to protest ending animal-based research.

CEP finds that many animal rights proponents, however, do not oppose responsible research for medical purposes. In rating companies for this guide, we have indicated with a "○" those companies that manufacture drugs and/or surgical equipment.

Companies do listen to consumers' concerns. If you care about this issue, here are some things you can do:

- Ask companies from which you buy cosmetics, household products or pharmaceuticals to report what they've done to promote alternatives to animal testing.
- Ask the companies from which you buy meat what they are doing to improve the quality of life for farm animals.
- Ask legislators to provide you with reports on what the regulatory agencies are doing to promote non-animal alternative testing.
- Become a vegetarian.
- Shop for a better world by selecting products made by companies rated ✔, ✔∗, ✔○, or ✔⊛.

SHOPPING FOR OUR RIGHT TO KNOW

Consumers, investors, employees and non-profit groups working in the public interest all need access to facts and figures in order to form knowledgeable opinions about corporations. A company's willingness to share information on its basic operations and its social endeavors is essential to this effort, and is an indication of corporate good citizenship.

Until recently, most corporations have resisted providing comparable data on social initiatives. Attempts to require companies to do so by law have been largely unsuccessful.

Though a majority of firms still do not publish information on social initiatives, many companies with a definite commitment to social responsibility have made it a priority to inform the public of the social impact of their operations.

More and more companies are adding a small section to their annual report discussing their "commitment" or "public responsibility." Other companies publish more extensive reports. Many of these reports are full of feel-good pictures and words but provide little substantive information on the company's social programs. The best ones document company efforts, demonstrate results and use comparable data for comparison.

Of the 168 companies rated in this book, 62 cooperated fully by providing extensive information on their social programs, 91 provided more limited information, and 15 gave us little or no information.

"About the Research" (at the back of the book) tells how we gathered information.

Let companies know that you want to know about their social performance:

- Ask companies that did not cooperate to provide information for our 1991 edition. Addresses appear on page 242.
- Urge members of Congress and the Securities and Exchange Commission to require disclosure of comparable data on corporate social performance.
- Encourage companies to publish meaningful social responsibility reports.
- Select products made by companies rated ✔.

SHOPPING FOR A THRIVING COMMUNITY

Walk through any community in America and you catch its spirit right away. Do a little checking and you may discover that the town's persona may be influenced by the major companies in the area.

The lack of affordable housing for low- and middle-income families and of quality public education have caused a stir in communities across the nation. The corporate community has heard and begun to respond with innovative community outreach programs.

Companies can support low-cost housing in a variety of ways: the construction of new housing, the refurbishment of existing housing, or, the revitalization of entire neighborhoods. Corporations can also contact experienced intermediaries for help in evaluating local housing needs.

The Local Initiatives Support Corporation (LISC), the Enterprise Foundation (EF), and the National Equity Fund (NEF) are three such intermediaries. They act as financial intermediaries, distributing corporate funds to local community organizations. Their work is having a large impact. For example, LISC has collaborated with over 400 community groups on the development of over 10,000 housing units. EF has worked with local groups in 27 cities and has created 2,900 affordable dwellings for the very poor since 1981.

By staking these organizations with grants, companies provide housing and also aid their workforce. Affordable housing near company workplaces aids in both recruitment and retainment of employees. Employee productivity is also positively affected because workers don't have to worry about travelling time and expenses. However, companies have realized that without at least a minimally educated pool of workers to choose from, the proximity of residences to the workplace will not matter. That is the key reason business is stepping into the classrooms.

Our education system is severely crippled. Students are either graduating from schools without basic skills or not graduating at all. As a result, communities are clamoring for mass overhaul of the system. The federal government has thus far been unwilling to increase substantially its commitment to education. Spending by the Department of Education, as a percentage of total federal outlays, has actually fallen from 2.5% in 1979 to 1.7% in 1988. the corporate community, is responding with imaginative programs. Although small in comparison even with federal and certainly with local government support of education, corporate Adopt-A-School, literacy projects, vocational training, employment programs, and volunteer and tutoring projects make a big difference. With these programs, companies hope to breathe new life into the school system they depend on.

Adopt-A-School is a fine example of a program that brings the corporate world and the community together, while giving neither control over the other. A business tries to prepare students for the job market by supplying public schools with updated equipment and placing some of its employees in these institutions as instructors or counselors.

A company's greatest resource is it employees. Volunteerism is a positive way to help the community and a visible way to help the company's name. Through executive help, work release for other employees, grants to organizations for which employees volunteer, job banks, and involvement of retired employees, communities receive much help to address local problems.

Not all corporations, however, are community minded. Many companies abandon towns which have been dependent on them or lay off large numbers of employees without adequate notice or retraining programs. Some companies are engaged in union busting. You can avoid buying from them.

To make your community a better and brighter place, you can:

- Volunteer at a community center, public interest group or school.
- Encourage your employer to establish a volunteer program.
- Join a local organization promoting housing and economic development efforts in your community.
- Write to companies to find out what kind of community outreach programs they support. Addresses on page 242.
- Consider a career in community work.
- Support companies rated ✔.

SHOPPING FOR
ENERGY ALTERNATIVES

Safe, clean, and cheap. Nuclear power sounded promising at first. The result has been quite different.

In the early seventies, nuclear power was widely considered the ideal answer to our heightened energy needs. But since 1978, not a single new nuclear plant has been ordered in the U.S. because of safety and reliability questions and high cost. Accumulated nuclear waste poses another serious problem.

It is very clear that of all the alternatives to coal and oil now feasible (nuclear, solar geothermal, hydroelectric, biomass, wind), energy conservation and improvements in energy efficiency are by far the cheapest and least harmful to workers, neighboring communities and the environment.

— By year-end 1989, nearly 190 publicly-held utilities in the U.S. were spending a total of $1 billion a year on conservation, according to the Investor Responsibility Research Center. Even the electric utility industry admits these expenditures will save 21,000 Megawatts, equal to the output of 21 large nuclear plants whose construction would have totalled $10 **billion** a year (assuming a 10-year building period).

— The Rocky Mountain Institute, a leader in the study of energy efficiency, reports that since 1979, the U.S. has obtained seven times as much new energy from energy savings as from *all* net increases in energy supply. As a result, our annual national energy bill is $150 billion smaller.

We need a sensible national energy policy that encourages appropriate technologies where they can be most useful. Almost 9% of our energy already comes from renewable sources, such as burning organic material and hydropower, according to the Environmental Defense Fund. Federal policy must also encourage new approaches — through incentives, investment tax credits, or mandatory minimum standards. These include the installation of maximum efficiency equipment and fixtures in new building construction, the use of cogeneration (the steam from fuel burned for heating is captured to spin turbines to generate electricity) where appropriate in industrial plants, and a firm improvement in fuel efficiency standards for new cars.

There are many ways you can contribute to energy conservation:

- Homeowners should take efficiency into consideration when buying new equipment and fixtures like windows, boilers, furnaces, air conditioners, insulation. The extra cost for maximum efficiency will be paid off through savings of fuel, electricity and water costs within a few years.
- Use fluorescent light bulbs. An 18-watt compact fluorescent bulb is equivalent to a 75-watt incandescent, lasts ten times as long, and saves $20 to $40 over the bulb's lifetime. You can now buy fluorescents that screw into regular sockets.
- Use public transportation, ride a bicycle, or walk whenever possible. If you must drive to work, join or form a carpool.
- Recycle. Not only is this good for the environment, it saves energy too. According to the Natural Resources Defense Council, each ton of recycled paper saves 20 trees eight meters high and 14 centimeters wide. Recycling a ton of glass saves 37 liters of oil.
- Weatherize your home; go slow on air-conditioning and heat; and look for low-energy, biodegradable packaging like paper and cardboard.
- If you agree with nuclear power advocates, select products made by companies rated ''Yes.''
- If you want to avoid involvement with nuclear power's safety risks and high cost, select products made by companies rated ''No.''

SHOPPING TO END APARTHEID

South Africa's apartheid is a system that enables a small
White minority to maintain political, social and economic control of the Black majority. While abuse of human
rights and exploitation of workers occurs in many countries, like Chile, China and Haiti, South Africa is the
sole nation where segregation is upheld by law and in
which the policies of U.S. companies are verifiably
documented. The Whites (only 16% of the population)
dictate where people of color may live, work or go to
school. They control what quality of education and
health care the Blacks receive (poor) and the mode of
transportation they use. Black South Africans cannot
vote in national elections, hold national office, own
guns or exercise basic political rights within the White
system.

Only recently has the rest of the world responded to
this offensive form of racism. In 1977, the Reverend
Leon Sullivan, president of The International Foundation for Education and Self Help and a director on
General Motors' board, responded to a plea by black
leaders in South Africa to form a code of conduct for
U.S. companies operating in their country. Hundreds of
companies signed on, often under stockholder pressure.
Later, stringent monitoring of compliance was introduced. These guidelines, which supported the rights
of people of color in the workplace and aimed to end
apartheid, became known as the Sullivan Principles.

Signators of the Sullivan Principles introduced, then upgraded progressive policies in South Africa. But a decade later, the Rev. Sullivan felt his goal of ending apartheid was nowhere in sight. In 1986, he renounced the principles and called for complete withdrawal of all U.S. companies from South Africa unless apartheid was essentially abolished by May 1987.

Then Congress passed the U.S. Comprehensive Anti-Apartheid Act of 1986, prohibiting new investment in South Africa and providing an economic disincentive: companies remaining can no longer receive U.S. tax credits for taxes paid to the South African government. In effect, that provision imposes a 70% tax rate on the companies' South African earnings. By June 1989, 186 of the 270 U.S. companies in South Africa (in 1984) had pulled out entirely or partially.

The companies were usually sold to South African partnerships. Some gave shares to black workers. The parent companies no longer directly support apartheid by paying taxes in South Africa. As a condition of their departure, some companies invested huge sums in the new South African entities, and their products are still available. Some left charitable foundations to aid black South Africans.

Some U.S. corporations still operating in South Africa feel they can make progress in human rights and support the Black community there only if they maintain their economic ties. They argue that Japanese companies will step right in if they leave. The Statement of Principles, formerly the Sullivan Principles, still monitors these companies. In 1988 there were 70 signatories. All but three companies in this guide that operate in South Africa have earned the top rating for compliance with the Statement of Principles. That means they are making good progress in enforcing nonsegregation in the workplace, equal and fair employment of all employees, equal pay, developing training programs for better jobs, increasing the number of people of color in management and supervisory positions, and improving the quality of employees' lives in housing, transportation, schooling, recreation and health facilities.

European companies also use a code of conduct. However, compliance is not independently monitored.

You can make a difference:

- Write to companies rated "Yes." Ask them to divest fully or to improve their practices under the Statement of Principles. Addresses are on page 242.
- Support community funds, housing funds and educational exchanges for Black South Africans.
- Write to urge your Senator or Representative to impose stricter sanctions on South Africa.
- Find out if your community is one of a growing number of localities that restrict purchasing from companies doing business in South Africa. If not, advocate it.
- Don't buy krugerrands.
- Buy products whose makers say "No" to apartheid.

SHOPPING FOR A CLEANER WORLD

The most truly global issue of today and tomorrow, the health of planet Earth, affects people of all races and income levels around the world. The threats to our planet's health come from a wide variety of sources: industrial, governmental and individual. Solutions — and there will have to be many — will demand innovation, compromise, flexibility and sacrifice from business, governments and citizens alike.

One of the most encouraging business trends is the increasing sensitivity of some consumer products companies to the environmental impacts of their products. "Green" products have been on the market for years in Europe, and are just now being introduced in Canada and the U.S. A recent report by Marketing Intelligence Service claims that 706 new "green" packaged goods have been introduced since 1984, including organically grown foods and beverages, products with bio- or photo-degradable packaging, detergents and cleaners with few or no phosphates, and products formulated without animal testing or animal ingredients or by-products. These products help cut down on solid waste, pollution, and the degradation of non-renewable resources.

Thus, some household products makers have begun packaging their detergents in recycled plastic (varying from 30% to 100% recycled resin); some have introduced pouches of concentrate that can be mixed with water in containers the consumer already has at home (using 85% less packaging). Several paper products companies offer bathroom tissue and paper towels unbleached with dioxin-forming chlorine; coffee filters made from natural unbleached paper pulp are available. Some of the larger consumer products companies cited in this guide are beginning to introduce such products on a test basis. Small companies founded on environmental principles are growing by leaps and bounds.

While many changes still have to be made at the policy level, it is clear that companies and government are responding to consumer pressure about environmental issues. There is a great deal you can do. Because over 90% of the 1989 **SHOPPING FOR A BETTER WORLD** buyers rated Environment as a top priority, we have made a long list:

- Conserve energy and make sure household equipment and fixtures are maximally efficient in their use of fuel, electricity and water. Weatherize your home to reduce heating and cooling needs. See **SHOPPING FOR ENERGY ALTERNATIVES.**

- Reuse containers and products as often as possible.

- Buy as few disposable items as possible.

- Recycle newspapers, bottles and cans. Millions of tons of cheap raw materials are wasted by being buried or burned. The Environmental Protection Agency estimates that 70 percent of all incinerator ash is glass and metals, which we should be recovering.

- If your community does not have a recycling program, ask officials to start one.

- Buy fresh food. It is usually more nutritious and uses less packaging.

- Don't buy products with excessive packaging.

- Look for paper packaging. It is easier on the environment than plastic, and both are safer than polystyrene or plastics mixed with other materials. Mixed materials are nearly impossible to recycle.

- Look for packaging that bears the recycled or recyclable symbol.
- Bring a canvas or nylon mesh bag to the store to save bags.
- Refuse to take extra, unnecessary shopping bags, especially plastic ones.
- Let stores and manufacturers know how you feel about needless packaging, the importance of recycling, organically-grown foods, and all-natural ingredients.
- Plant your own organic vegetable garden. Use waste vegetables scraps for your compost.
- Use natural alternatives to household cleaners, polishes, bug sprays, and solvents. Try baking soda and vinegar for cleaning.
- Plant trees. Trees turn CO_2 into oxygen. One tree can replace up to 48 pounds of carbon a year. Trees prevent erosion and desertification, and offset the greenhouse effect. Well-placed trees around a house can lower air-conditioning needs by 10 to 50 percent.
- Avoid products containing CFCs, such as: cleaning sprays for sewing machines, VCRs, and electronic equipment; aerosol dust-removers for cameras; rigid insulation; and foam packaging. Unfortunately, some of these products have no workable substitute.
- If your car has air conditioning, make sure it's well sealed. The single largest source of CFC emissions is from leaky car air conditioners. An increasing number of shops will capture and recycle these CFCs.
- Don't use unnecessary dry cleaning since the process adds hazardous chemicals to the water system.
- Turn off lights when you leave the room.
- Ask for organically-grown food.
- Use fans and open windows rather than air conditioning.
- Buy products made by companies rated ✔ in this guide.

SHOPPING FOR FAMILY BENEFITS

Corporate response to the needs of the family has improved dramatically in the last decade. Today, companies offer a variety of family benefits such as parental leave, flextime, job sharing, child and/or dependent care assistance, and flexible benefits. Gains have been particularly strong in the crucial area of child care. In 1978, only 110 companies offered any form of child care assistance. Four years later, the number of firms had quintupled to 600. At present, some 4,177 companies provide their employees with one or more of these benefits. Yet the availability and affordabilty of child care remains woefully inadequate. According to the Bureau of Labor Statistics, almost 40% of all companies with more than 10 employees do not provide family benefits of any kind.

The responsiveness of many companies has been more reactive than proactive. Many changes are occurring in response to new policies in 18 states that require businesses to have some kind of family and medical leave policy. However, the government's influence is not the only motivating force; other factors include a new understanding of the changing composition of the workforce and the economic impact of outdated policies that ignore family responsibilities.

The composition of the workforce today is radically different from 40 years ago. Today, for instance, 70% of the women in the child-bearing years of 25 to 34 have jobs, double the number that did in 1950. This shift is forcing many companies to readjust their benefits to meet the needs of their new employees. Companies are becoming more aware of the economic impact of their practices as well. It was common at one time for employers to fire and replace pregnant employees. This proved to be more expensive than granting leave time to already qualified and well-trained employees.

The great influx of child-bearing women into the workforce has meant that the most offered and studied family benefit is parental or maternal leave. Women make up 44% of the total labor force and over 80% of those women will become pregnant in their working lives. A recent study, of 3,850 employers by the National Council of Jewish Women, Center for the Child, indicated that 51% of the smaller companies (less than 20 workers) and 72% of the larger companies offer at least eight weeks for maternity leave. Some exceptional companies allow much more. A few companies offer the same amount of leave time off for situations, such as adoption, fostercare, or stepchildren.

The United States is far behind other countries in terms of family benefits. 127 countries, including Japan and most of Europe, require parental or maternal leave. However, Congress is currently considering the ABC Bill (Act for Better Child Care), which proposes child care subsidies for low and middle income families, funding for additional child care facilities and staff and establishing nation-wide safety standards for the child care industry.

Whether you are a parent or not, you can work for a better chance for America's children:

- Urge your local Congressional Representative and Senator to support the ABC Bill.
- Ask what you or your employer can do to improve the life of a child with better family benefits like leave time, day care, scholarships and child care assistance.
- Volunteer at a child care center or a homebound program for the elderly.
- Promote family or medical leave legislation in your home state.
- Consider a career in teaching or early childhood education.
- Buy products from companies with good family policies, indicated by a ✔.

RATINGS FOR
THE COMPANIES

BIG COMPANIES (OVER 100 EMPLOYEES)

Company	Abbr.	$	♀	✊	🕊	♨	⚛	🐇	🌐	ALERT
Abbott Laboratories	ABT	✗	✓	?	No	✗○	✓	No	Yes●	✓	infant formula
Alberto-Culver	ACV	?	✓	?	No	✗	?	No	No	?	
Allied-Lyons PLC	ALP	?	?	?	No	✗	?	No	Yes†	?	
American Brands	AMB	✓	✓	✗	No	✓	?	No	Yes	✓	cigarettes
American Cyanamid	ACY	✓	✓	?	No	✗○	✓	No	Yes*	✓	makes pesticides
American Home Products	AHP	✗	✓	✗	No	✓(*)	✓	No	Yes*	✗	infant formula
Anheuser-Busch	BUD	✓+	✓	✓	No	✓	✓	No	No	✓	
Archer Daniels Mdlnd. Co.	ADM	?	?	?	No	?	?	No	No	✗	
Avon	AVP	✓	✓	✓	No	✓	✓	No	No	✓	
Beatrice Company	BTC	✓+	✓	✓	No	✗○	✓	No	No	✓	
Beecham Group PLC	BECH	?	✓	?	No	?	?	No	Yes†	✓	

Company	Abbr.	$	♀		✈			⚛			ALERT
Ben & Jerry's	B&J	✔+	✔	✗	No	✔	✔	No	✔	✔	1% For Peace
Borden	BN	✗	✔	✔	No	✓	✓	Yes●	✓	✓	
Bristol-Myers	BMY	✔	✔	✔	No	✓(*)	✔	Yes*	?	✗	infant formula
Cadbury Schweppes Inc.	CADB	✓	✗	✓	No	✓	✓	Yes†	?	✔	
Campbell Soup	CPB	✓	✔	✓	No	?	✓	No	✔	✔	on-site daycare
Carme	CARM	?	✓	✓	No	?	?	Yes	✔	✓	
Carter-Wallace	CAR	?	✗	✗	No	✗○	✗	No	✓	?	
Castle & Cooke	CKE	?	✗	?	No	?	✗	No	?	?	pesticide use
Celestial Seasonings	CS	?	✔	✔	No	✔*	✔	No	✔	✗	
Church & Dwight	CRCH	?	✓	?	No	✓	✓	No	✔	✓	

✔ = Top Rating   ✓ = Middle Rating   ✗ = Bottom Rating   ? = Insufficient Information
For a more detailed explanation see key on page 10

Page 43

BIG COMPANIES

Company	Abbr.	$	(symbol)	(symbol)	(symbol)	(symbol)	(symbol)	⚛	(symbol)	(symbol)	ALERT
Clorox	CLX	✓	✓	✓	No	✓	✓	No	✓	✓	
Coca-Cola	KO	✓	✓	✓	No	✓	✓	Yes	✓	✓	
Colgate-Palmolive	CL	✓+	✓	✓	No	✓*	✓	Yes*	✓	✓	
ConAgra	CAG	?	?	?	No	✗	?	?	?	?	OSHA fines
Coors, Adolph	ACC	✓+	✓	✓	No	✓	✓	No	✓	✓	
CPC International	CPC	✗	✓	✓	No	✓	✓	No	✓	✓	
Curtice-Burns	CBI	✓+	?	✓	No	✓	✓	No	?	✓	
Dean Foods	DF	?	?	?	No	?	?	No	✗	✗	
Di Giorgio Corporation	DIG	?	?	?	No	✓(*)	?	No	?	✗	
Dow Chemical Co.	DOW	✓	✓	✓	No	✓(*)	✓	Yes	✓	✓	makes pesticides
Eastman Kodak	EK	✓	✓	✓	Yes	✗	✓	No	✓	✓	
Faberge, Inc.	FAB	?	?	?	No	?	?	No	✓	?	

BIG COMPANIES

Company	Abbr.	💲	⚥	✊	✈	🐴	⚛	🌐	♻	ALERT
First Brands	FB	?	?	?	No	?	?	No	?	✗	
Flowers Industries	FLO	?	✗	✓	No	?	?	No	?	✗	
General Electric	GE	✓	✓	✓	Yes*	✗	✓	Yes	✗	✓	INFACT boycott
General Mills	GIS	✓+	✓	✓	No	✓	✓	No	✗	✓	
Georgia-Pacific	GP	?	✓	✓	No	✓	✓	No	✗	✗	
Gerber Products	GEB	?	✓	✓	No	✓	✓	No	?	✓	clearcutting
Gillette	GS	✓	✓	✓	No	✗	✓	No	Yes●	✓	
Grand Metropolitan PLC	GMP	?	?	?	?	✗	?	Yes†	?	?	dolphins caught
Greyhound Corp.	G	?	?	✓	No	✓	✓	No	?	?	
GTE	GTE	✗	✓	✓	Yes*	✓	✓	No	✓	✓	

✓ = Top Rating   √ = Middle Rating   ✗ = Bottom Rating   ? = Insufficient Information
For a more detailed explanation see key on page 10

BIG COMPANIES

Company	Abbr.	💲	⚥		✈		⚛		🌐	ALERT
Heinz, H.J.	HNZ	✓	✗	✓	No	✓	No	✓	✓	dolphins caught
Hershey Food Corp.	HSY	✓	✓	✓	No	✓	No	✓	✓	
Holly Farms Corp.	HFF	?	✗	?	No	?	No	✗	?	
Hormel, George A.	HRL	✓	✓	✓	No	✗	No	✓	✗	labor disputes
Iroquois Brands	IBC	?	✓	✓	No	?	No	?	✗	
James River Corp.	JR	✓	✓	?	No	✓	No	✓	✓	
John B. Sanfilippo & Son	JSAN	?	✓	✗	No	✓	No	✓	✓	
Johnson & Johnson	JNJ	✓	✓	✓	No	✓(*)	Yes*	✓	✓	
Johnson Products	JPC	?	✓	?	No	?	No	✓	✗	
Johnson & Son, S.C.	SCJ	✓+	✓	✓	No	✓	Yes●	✓	✓	1st to ban CFC's
Kellogg	K	✓	✓	✓	No	?	Yes●	✓	✓	
Kimberly-Clark	KMB	✗	✓	✗	No	?	Yes●	✗	?	disposable diapers

Company	Abbr.	💲	♀	✈	🏃	✊	🐾	⚛	🔬	🐇	ALERT
Loma Linda Foods	LOMA	?	✓	No	✓	✓	✗	No	No	✓	✗	
Mars	MARS	?	?	No	✓	✗	?	No	No	?	✗	
McCormick & Co.	MCRK	✔+	✓	No	✓	?	✓	No	No	✓	✗	
Mead Corporation	MEA	✔	✓	No	?	✓	✓	No	Yes	✓	✗	clearcutting
Miles Labs	MILS	?	?	No	✗○	✓*	✓	No	Yes†	?	✗	
Minnesota Mining & Manu.	MMM	✓	✓	No	✓*	✓	✓	No	Yes*	✓	✓	
Nestle S.A.	NEST	?	✓	No	?	✓	✓	No	Yes†	✓	✓	infant formula
Noxell	NOXL	✔+	✓	No	✓	✗	✗	No	No	✓	✗	
Ocean Spray Cranberries	OSC	?	?	No	?	✓	✓	No	No	✗	?	
PepsiCo	PEP	✔	✓	No	?	✓	✓	No	Yes	✓	✓	

✔ = Top Rating ✓ = Middle Rating ✗ = Bottom Rating ? = Insufficient Information

For a more detailed explanation see key on page 10

BIG COMPANIES

Company	Abbr.	$	⚥	(icon)	✈	(icon)	(icon)	⚛	(icon)	(icon)	ALERT
Pfizer	PFE	✓	✓	✓	No	✓(*)	✓	No	✓	✗	heart-valve suit
Philip Morris	MO	✗	✓+	✓	No	?	?	Yes	✗	?	cigarettes
Polaroid	PRD	✓	✓	✓	No	✓	✓	No	✓	✓	
Procter & Gamble	PG	✓	✓	✓	No	✓(*)	✓	No	✓	✓	disposable diapers
Quaker Oats	OAT	✓	✓	✓	No	✓	✓	Yes	✓	✓	
Ralston Purina	RAL	✗	✓	✓	No	✓	✓	No	✓	✗	dolphins caught
Revlon	REVL	?	?	?	No	✓	?	Yes●	✓	✓	
Reynold's Metals	RLM	✗	✗	✗	No	✓	✓	No	✓	✗	
RJR Nabisco	RJR	✓	✓	✓	No	?	?	Yes*	✓	✗	cigarettes
Rorer	ROR	?	?	✗	No	✗○	✓	No	?	?	
Sara Lee	SLE	✓	✓	✓	No	✓	✓	Yes	✓	✓	
Schering-Plough	SGP	✓	✓	✓	No	✓(*)	✓	Yes●	✓	✓	

Company	Abbr.	$	♀					☢				ALERT
Scott Paper	SPP	◐	✓	✓	No	✗	✓	No	No	✗	✓	forestry criticized
Seagram Co. Ltd., The	VO	?	?	◐	No	◐	?	No	No	◐	◐	
Smucker, J.M.	SJM	◐	✗	◐	No	?	◐	No	No	✓	✗	
Solgar Company	SLGR	?	?	?	No	?	◐	No	No	?	?	
Squibb	SQB	?	◐	✓	No	✗○	◐	No	Yes●	?	◐	
Tasty Baking Co.	TBC	✓+	◐	✓	No	✓	✓	No	No	✓	◐	
Tillamook Cheese	TILA	✗	✗	✓	No	?	?	No	No	✗	✗	
Topps Chewing Gum	TOPP	?	✗	◐	No	?	?	No	No	✓	?	
Twin Laboratories	TWIN	?	✓	✓	No	✓	✓	No	No	◐	✗	
Tyson Foods	TYSN	?	✗	◐	No	✗	◐	No	No	◐	✗	

✓ = Top Rating ◐ = Middle Rating ✗ = Bottom Rating ? = Insufficient Information
For a more detailed explanation see key on page 10

BIG COMPANIES

BIG COMPANIES

Company	Abbr.	💲	⚥		✈	🤝		⚛				ALERT
Unilever N.V.	UN	✗	✓	✓	No	✓*	✗	No	Yes†	?	?	
Und. Biscuits (Hlds.) PLC	UBH	?	?	?	No	✓	?	No	No	?	✗	
United Brands	UB	✓	✓	✓	No	✓	✗	No	No	?	✓	labor disputes
Universal Foods Corp.	UFC	✓	✓	✗	No	✓	?	No	No	?	?	
Upjohn	UPJ	✓	✓	✓	No	✗○	✓	No	Yes●	✓	✓	
Warner-Lambert	WLA	✓	✓	✓	No	✗○	✓	No	Yes●	✓	✓	
Whitman Industries	WH	✓	✓	✓	No	✓○	✗	No	No	?	✓	
Wilson Foods Corp.	WF	?	?	?	No	✓	?	No	No	?	✗	
Wrigley, Wm.	WWY	?	?	✓	No	✗	?	No	No	?	?	

SMALL COMPANIES (100 OR FEWER EMPLOYEES)

Company	Abbr.	💲	⚥		✈	🤝		⚛				ALERT
21st Century Foods#	TFC	✗	✓	✓	No	✓	?	No	No		✓	
American Health Pdcts.#	AMH	?	?	No		✓	✗	No	No		?	✗

Company	Abbr.	$	♀	✈	🏊	⚛	🐾			🌐	ALERT
Apple & Eve#	APNE	?	✗	No	✓	✓	?	No	No	?	✗
Aroma Vera#	AV	?	✓	✓	✓	✓	?	No	No	✓	✗
Arrowhead Mills Inc.*	AM	?	✗	✓	✓	✓	?	No	No	✓	✓
Associated Cooperatives#	ACOP	?	✓	No	✓	✓	✓	No	No	✓	✓
Aubrey Organics#	AUB	?	✓	✓	✓	✓	✓	No	No	✓	✓
Aura Cacia#	AURA	?	✓	✓	✓	✓	✓	No	No	✓	✓
Autumn Harp#	AUT	?	✗	No	✓	✓	?	No	No	✓	✗
Barbara's Bakery#	BARB	?	✓	No	✓	✓	✓	No	No	✓	✗
Brown Cow West Corp.*	BCWC	?	?	No	✓	✓	✗	No	No	✓	✓
Cherry Hill Coop. Cannery.#	CHER	?	✓	No	✓	✓	?	No	No	✓	?

✓ = Top Rating   ✓ = Middle Rating   ✗ = Bottom Rating   ? = Insufficient Information

For a more detailed explanation see key on page 10

SMALL COMPANIES

SMALL COMPANIES

Company	Abbr.	💲	♀♂	✈	⚒	⚛	🐾	🏠	ALERT
Deer Valley Farm#	DVF	✗	✓	No	✓	✓	No	✓	✗
Dolefam#	DFAM	?	✓	No	✓	✓	No	✓	✓
Eden Foods#	EDEN	✗	✗	No	✓	✓	No	✓	✗
Falcon Trading Co.#	FALC	?	✓	No	✓	✓	No	✓	✓
Fantastic Foods, Inc.#	FFI	?	✓	No	✓	✗	No	✓	✗
Garden of Eatin'#	GEAT	?	?	No	✓	✓	No	✓	✗
Great Eastern Sun#	GES	?	✓	No	✓	✗	No	✓	✗
Health Valley Nat. Foods#	HVAL	?	✓	No	?	?	No	✓	✗
Homestyle Foods#	HOME	?	✓	No	✗	?	No	✓	✗
Imagine Foods#	IF	?	✓	No	✓	✓	No	✓	✓
Kanoa: A Free Spirit#	KFS	?	✓	No	✗	✗	No	✓	✗
Klaire Labs#	KLAB	?	✓	No	✓	✓	No	✓	✗

Company	Abbr.	$	♀	⚥	⚛	🔫	🌐	🐾	☣	ALERT
Lifetone International#	LFTI	?	✗	No	✓	No	No	✓	?	
Loriva Supreme Foods#	LOR	?	?	No	✓	No	?	?	?	
Mayacamas Fine Foods#	MAYA	?	?	No	✓	No	?	?	✗	
Modern Products#	MOD	?	?	No	✓	✓	No	?	?	
Mountain Ocean#	MOUN	?	✓	No	✓	✗	No	✓	✗	
Murdock International#	MUR	?	✗	No	✓	✗	No	?	?	
Natura Foods#	NFS	?	?	No	✓	✓	No	✓	?	
Nature's Herbs#	HERB	?	✗	No	✓	✗	No	✓	?	
Newman's Own#	NEWO	✓+	✓	No	✓	✓	No	✓	✓	profit to charity
Orjene Natural Cosmetics#	ORJ	?	?	No	✓	?	No	✓	✗	

✓ = Top Rating   √ = Middle Rating   ✗ = Bottom Rating   ? = Insufficient Information

For a more detailed explanation see key on page 10

SMALL COMPANIES

Company	Abbr.	💲	⚥	✈	🏞	🤝	⚛	🐾	✡	ALERT
Paul Penders#	PP	?	✓	No	✓	✓	No	✓	✓	
Rachel Perry Inc.#	RP	✗	✓	No	✓	✓	No	◐	✗	
Reviva Labs#	REV	?	✓	No	✓	◐	No	◐	✗	
San-J International#	SANJ	?	✓	No	✓	✓	No	✓	✗	
Tom's of Maine#	TOM	✓+	✓	No	✓	✓	No	✓	◐	
Universal Labs#	ULAB	?	◐	No	◐	?	No	◐	✗	
Vegetarian Health#	VH	?	?	No	◐	?	No	?	?	
GAS AND OIL COMPANIES										
Amoco	AN	◐	✓	Yes	✗	✓	No	◐	✓	
ARCO	ARC	◐	✓	Yes	✗	✓	No	✗	✗	
Atlantic Richfield	ARC	◐	✓	Yes	✗	✓	No	✗	✓	
BP America	BP	?	◐	No	◐	✓	Yes†	✗	✓	

Company	Abbr.	💲	⚥	✈	🐾	🐎	☢	🏭	🏡	ALERT
Chevron	CHV	✓	✗	Yes	✓	✓	No	Yes*	✗	✓	makes pesticides
Exxon	XON	✗	✓	Yes*	✓*	✓	No	No	✗	✓	oil spill
Getty	QTX	?	✓	Yes	✓	✗	No	Yes*	✗	✓	worst plant for air
Marathon	X	?	✗	No	✓	✗	No	No	✗	✗	
Mobil	MOB	?	✓	Yes	✓	✗	No	No	✗	✓	
Phillips Petroleum	P	✓	✓	No	✓	✓	No	No	✓	✓	
Phillips 66	P	✓	✓	No	✓	✓	No	No	✓	✓	
Shell Oil Company, USA	SC	✓	✓	Yes	✓*	✓	No	Yes†	✗	✓	
Sun	SUN	?	?	No	✓	?	No	No	✗	✗	
Sunoco	SUN	?	?	No	✓	?	No	No	✗	✗	

✓ = Top Rating   ✓ = Middle Rating   ✗ = Bottom Rating   ? = Insufficient Information

For a more detailed explanation see key on page 10

GAS AND OIL COMPANIES

Company	Abbr.	$	♀	🌲	🤝	⚛	🐾	☢	🐇	♻	ALERT
Texaco	QTX	?	✓	✗	Yes	✓	✗	No	Yes*	✗	✓	worst plant for air
USX	X	?	✗	✗	No	✓	✗	No	No	✗	✗	
SUPERMARKETS												
A&P	GAP	?	✓	✓	No	✓	✓	No	No	✗	✓	refuses cans
Acme Markets, Inc.	ASC	?	✓	✓	No	✓	?	No	?	?	?	
Albertson's, Inc.	ABS	?	✓	?	No	✓	?	No	?	?	?	
Alpha Beta Stores	ASC	?	✓	✓	No	✓	?	No	?	?	?	
American Stores	ASC	?	✓	✓	No	✓	?	No	?	?	?	
American Superstores, Inc.	ASC	?	✓	✓	No	✓	?	No	?	?	?	
Bruno's Inc.	BRI	?	✓	?	No	✓	?	No	?	✗	?	
Bursil, Inc.	GF	?	✓	✓	No	✓	?	No	?	✗	?	
H. E. Butt Grocery	HEBG	?	?	?	No	✓	?	No	?	?	✓	

Company	Abbr.	💲	♀	✈	👥	⚛	🤝	🕊	ALERT
Buttrey Food Stores	ASC	?	✔	✔	No	√	No	?	?	
Dillon Companies, Inc.	ASC	?	✔	✔	No	√	No	?	?	
Dominick's Finer Foods	DOM	?	?	✔	No	√	No	?	?	
Expo. Stores, Inc.	VON	?	√	?	No	√	No	√	?	removed tobacco
Food Lion	FL	?	?	?	No	√	No	?	✔	
Fred Meyer, Inc.	MEYR	?	?	?	No	√	No	?	✗	
Giant Eagle	GIA	?	√	?	No	√	No	?	√	
Giant Food, Inc.	GF	√	√	√	No	✗	No	?	✗	
Grand Union Company	GUC	?	?	?	No	√	Yes†	√	?	
Grt. Atlan. & Pacif. T. Co.	GAP	?	√	?	No	√	No	√	√	refuses cans

✔ = Top Rating   ✗ = Bottom Rating   √ = Middle Rating   ? = Insufficient Information

For a more detailed explanation see key on page 10

SUPERMARKETS

SUPERMARKETS

Company	Abbr.	💲	⚥	⚖	✈	🐾	🏭	⚛	🌸	☠	ALERT
Jewel Food Stores	ASC	?	✓	✓	No	✓	?	No	?	?	
The Kroger Co.	KR	✓	✓	✓	No	✓	✓	No	?	✗	
Leco, Inc.	GF	✓	✓	✓	No	✓	✓	No	?	✗	
Pathmark	SGH	?	✓	✓	No	✓	✓	No	✓	✓	
Publix Supermarkets	PUB	?	✓	✗	No	✓	?	No	✓	✗	
Purity Supreme	SGH	?	✓	✓	No	✓	✓	No	✓	✓	
Ralph's Grocery Co.	RG	?	✓	✗	No	?	✓	?	?	✗	
Safeway Stores, Inc.	SAFE	?	✓	✓	No	✓	✓	No	✓	✓	
Shaw Comm. Supermarket	GF	?	✓	✓	No	✓	✓	No	?	✗	
Skaggs	ASC	?	✓	✓	No	✓	?	No	?	?	
Smith's Fd./Drg. Cts., Inc.	SMC	?	✗	✓	No	✓	?	No	?	✗	
Star Market Co.	ASC	?	✓	✓	No	✓	?	No	?	?	

Company	Abbr.	(icon)	(icon)	(icon)	(icon)	(icon)	(icon)	(icon)	ALERT
Stop & Shop	STOP	?	✓	No	✗	?	No	✓	
Supmkts.Gen Hldgs.Corp.	SGH	?	✓	No	✓	✓	No	✓	
The Vons Companies, Inc.	VON	?	✓	No	✓	?	No	?	removed tobacco
Winn-Dixie Stores, Inc.	WIN	?	?	No	✗	?	No	?	

✓ = Top Rating   ✓ = Middle Rating   ✗ = Bottom Rating   ? = Insufficient Information

For a more detailed explanation see key on page 10

SUPERMARKETS

RATINGS BY PRODUCT

ALCOHOLIC BEVERAGES

Company or Product	Abbr.	💲	♀	✈	🌍	⚛				ALERT
ALCOHOLIC BEVERAGES										
Budweiser	BUD	✓+	✓	No	✓	✓	No	✓	✓	
Busch	BUD	✓+	✓	No	✓	✓	No	✓	✓	
Coors	ACC	✓+	✓	No	✓	✓	No	✓	✓	
Dewey Stevens	BUD	✓+	✓	No	✓	✓	No	✓	✓	
Elephant	BUD	✓+	✓	No	✓	✓	No	✓	✓	
LA	BUD	✓+	✓	No	✓	✓	No	✓	✓	
Leinenkugel	MO	✗	✓	No	?	✓	No	Yes	?	cigarettes
Lite	MO	✗	✓	No	?	✓	No	Yes	✗	?	cigarettes
Lowenbrau	MO	✗	✓	No	?	✓	No	Yes	✗	?	cigarettes

✓ = Top Rating   ✓ = Middle Rating   ✗ = Bottom Rating   ? = Insufficient Information

For a more detailed explanation see key on page 10

Page 61

ALCOHOLIC BEVERAGES

ALCOHOLIC BEVERAGES

Company or Product	Abbr.	💲	⚥	△	✈	✍	⚙	⚛	🌍	☁	ALERT
Magnum	MO	✗	✓	✓	No	?	✓	Yes	✗	?	cigarettes
Meister Brau	MO	✗	✓	✓	No	?	✓	Yes	✗	?	cigarettes
Michelob	BUD	✓+	✓	✓	No	✓	✓	No	✓	✓	
Miller	MO	✗	✓	✓	No	✓	✓	Yes	✗	?	cigarettes
Milwaukee's Best	MO	✗	✓	✓	No	?	✓	Yes	✗	?	cigarettes
Munich Oktoberfest	MO	✗	✓	✓	No	?	✓	Yes	✗	?	cigarettes
Natural Light	BUD	✓+	✓	✓	No	✓	✓	No	✓	✓	
Seagram's	VO	?	?	?	No	?	✓	No	✓	✓	
BABY FOODS											
Beechnut	NEST	?	?	?	No	?	✗	Yes†	✓	✓	infant formula
Enfamil	BMY	✓	✓	✓	No	✓(*)	✓	Yes*	✗	✓	infant formula
First Foods	GEB	?	?	✓	No	?	✓	No	✓	✓	

Company or Product	Abbr.	💲	⚢	[icon]	[icon]	⚛	[icon]	[icon]	[icon]	ALERT
Gerber	GEB	?	✓	No	✓	No	✓	?	✓	
Good Nature	NEST	?	?	No	✓	Yes†	?	?	✓	infant formula
i-soyalac	LOMA	?	✓	No	✓	No	✓	✓	✗	
Isomil	ABT	✗	✓	No	✗○	Yes●	✓	✓	✓	infant formula
Mead Johnson	BMY	✓	✓	No	✓✱	Yes✱	✓	?	✗	infant formula
Natura#	NFS	?	?	No	✓	No	✗	✓	?	
Nursoy	AHP	✗	✗	No	✓✱	Yes✱	✓	✓	✗	infant formula
Pro Sobee	BMY	✓	✓	No	✓✱	Yes✱	✓	?	✗	infant formula
Ross Laboratories	ABT	✗	✗	No	✗○	Yes●	✓	✓	✓	infant formula
S-M-A	AHP	✗	✗	No	✓✱	Yes✱	✓	✓	✗	infant formula

✓ = Top Rating   ⩗ = Middle Rating   ✗ = Bottom Rating   ? = Insufficient Information

For a more detailed explanation see key on page 10

BABY FOODS

Page 63

Company or Product	Abbr.	$	♀	🏃	🐟🌲	🐴	⚛	☁	🕊	⚖	ALERT
Similac	ABT	✗	✓	?	No	✗○	✓	No	Yes●	✓	✓	infant formula
soyalac	LOMA	?	✓	✓	No	✓	✗	No	No	✓	✗	
Wyeth-Ayerst	AHP	✗	✓	✗	No	✓(●)	✓	No	Yes*	✓	✗	infant formula
BAKING MIXES												
Arrowhead Mills#	AM	?	✓	✓	No	✓	?	No	No	✓	✓	
Aunt Jemima	OAT	✓	✓	✓	No	✓	✓	No	No	✓	✓	
Bake Shop	GIS	✓+	✓	✓	No	✓	✓	No	No	✓	✓	
Betty Crocker	GIS	✓+	✓	✓	No	✓	✓	No	No	✓	✓	
Bisquick	GIS	✓+	✓	✓	No	✓	✓	No	No	✓	✓	
Bundt	GMP	?	✓	?	No	✓	?	?	Yes†	?	?	dolphins caught
Duncan Hines	PG	✓	✓	✓	No	✓	✗	No	Yes	✓	✓	disposable diapers
Dutch Maid	K	✓	✓	✓	No	✓	✓	No	Yes●	✓	✓	

BAKING MIXES

Company or Product	Abbr.	🔬	💲	♀	✈	🐾	🎗	⚛	☢	🌐	☮	ALERT
Fearn Natural Foods#	MOD	?	?	?	No	✓	✓	No	?	✓	?	
Flako	OAT	✓	✓	✓	No	✓	✓	No	?	✓	✓	
Hansen Island	K	✓	✓	?	No	✓	✓	Yes●	✓	✓	✓	
Health Valley Nat. Foods #	HVAL	?	✓	✓	No	?	✓	No	✓	✓	✓	
Hungry Jack	GMP	?	?	?	?	✓	✗	Yes†	?	?	?	dolphins caught
Kraft	MO	✗	✓	✓	No	✓	✓	Yes	✗	✓	?	cigarettes
Microrave	GIS	✓+	✓	✓	No	✓	✓	No	✓	✓	✓	
Mother's Best	BTC	✓+	?	?	No	?	?	No	✗	✓	✓	
Mrs. Butterworth's	UN	✗	✓	✓	No	✓*	✓	Yes†	?	?	?	
Pepperidge Farm	CPB	✓	✓	✓	No	✓	✓	No	✓	✓	✓	on-site daycare

✓ = Top Rating   ✓ = Middle Rating   ✗ = Bottom Rating   ? = Insufficient Information

For a more detailed explanation see key on page 10

Page 65

Company or Product	Abbr.	$	⚥	◉	✈	🌍	✊	⚛	🐬	ALERT
Pillsbury	GMP	?	?	?	?	?	✗	Yes†	?	dolphins caught
Quick & Easy	AHP	✗	✓	✗	No	✓(*)	✓	Yes*	✗	infant formula
Rustco	HFF	?	✗	?	No	✓	?	No	?	
Super Moist	GIS	✓+	✓	✓	No	✓	✓	No	✓	
Toll House	NEST	?	?	?	No	?	✗	Yes†	✓	infant formula
White Lily	HFF	?	✗	?	No	?	✗	No	?	
BAKING NEEDS										
Amberex	UFC	?	✓	✓	No	✓	✓	No	?	
Argo	CPC	✗	✓	✓	No	✓	✓	No	✓	
Arm & Hammer	CRCH	?	?	?	No	✓*	✓	No	✓	
Baker's Joy	ACV	?	?	✗	No	✗	✗	No	?	
Baking Magic	MCRK	✓+	✓	✓	No	✓	?	No	✗	

Company or Product	Abbr.	$	⚥	✈	✊	🐾	⚛	◎	◍	ALERT
Betty Crocker	GIS	✔+	✔	No	✔	✔	No	No	✔	✔	
Cake-Mate	MCRK	✔+	√	No	✔	✔	No	No	√	✖	
Calumet	MO	✖	✔	No	?	✔	No	Yes	✖	?	cigarettes
Choco-Bake	NEST	?	✔	No	?	✖	No	Yes†	?	✔	infant formula
Cream	G	?	?	No	✔	√	No	No	√	?	
Crisco	PG	✔	✔	No	✔(*)	✔	No	Yes	√	✔	disposable diapers
Davis Baking Powder	RJR	✔	✔	No	?	✔	No	Yes*	✖	✖	cigarettes
Duncan Hines	PG	✔	✔	No	✔(*)	✔	No	Yes	√	✔	disposable diapers
El Molino#	AMH	?	?	No	✔	√	No	No	?	✖	
Festive Fixings	WF	?	?	No	?	√	No	No	?	✖	

✔ = Top Rating   √ = Middle Rating   ✖ = Bottom Rating   ? = Insufficient Information

For a more detailed explanation see key on page 10

Page 67

BAKING NEEDS

BAKING NEEDS

Company or Product	Abbr.	💲	👥	✊	✈	🐾	〰	☢	🕊	ALERT
Frosting Supreme	GMP	?	?	?	?	?	?	?	?	dolphins caught
Mazola	CPC	✗	✓	✓	No	✓	✓	No	✓	
McCormick	MCRK	✓+	✓	✓	No	✓	?	No	✓	
Mini-Morsels	GIS	✓+	✓	✗	No	✓	✓	No	✓	
Nestle	NEST	?	?	✗	No	?	✗	Yes†	✓	infant formula
PAM	AHP	✗	✓	✗	No	✓(*)	✓	Yes*	✗	infant formula
Pillsbury	GMP	?	?	✓	?	?	?	Yes†	?	dolphins caught
Quick-Rise	UFC	✓	✓	✗	No	✓	✓	No	?	
Rapidrise	RJR	✓	✓	✓	No	?	?	Yes*	✗	cigarettes
Red Star	UFC	✓	✓	✗	No	✓	?	No	?	
Taste Tone	UFC	✓	✓	✗	No	✓	?	No	?	
Toll House	NEST	?	?	?	No	?	✗	Yes†	✓	infant formula

Company or Product	Abbr.	💲	♀	(icon)	(icon)	(icon)	(icon)	(icon)	⚛	(icon)	(icon)	ALERT
Treasures	NEST	?	?	✗	No	?	✓	No	Yes†	?	✓	infant formula
Universal Labs#	ULAB	?	✓	?	No	✓	✓	No	No	✓	✗	
Weight Watchers	HNZ	✓	✓	✗	No	✓	✓	No	Yes	✓	✓	dolphins caught
Yeako	UFC	✓	✓	✗	No	✓	✓	No	No	?	?	
BREAD & TOAST												
Beefsteak	RAL	✗	✓	✗	No	✓	✓	No	No	✓	✗	dolphins caught
Bun Length	MO	✗	✓	✓	✓	?	✓	No	Yes	✗	?	cigarettes
Cobblestone Mill	FLO	?	✗	?	No	?	✓	No	No	?	✗	
Continental Baking Co.	RAL	✗	✓	✗	No	✓	✓	No	No	✓	✗	dolphins caught
Evangeline Maid	FLO	?	✗	?	No	?	?	No	No	?	✗	

✓ = Top Rating ✓ = Middle Rating ✗ = Bottom Rating ? = Insufficient Information

For a more detailed explanation see key on page 10

Page 69

BREAD & TOAST

Company or Product	Abbr.	💲	⚥	✈	🐾	♟	⚛	🐦	🌍	ALERT
Homepride	RAL	✗	✓	No	✓	✓	No	✓	✗	dolphins caught
Jane Parker	GAP	?	✓	No	✓	✓	No	✓	✓	refuses cans
Lender's Bagels	MO	✗	✓	No	?	✓	Yes	✗	?	cigarettes
Lifetone International#	LFTI	?	✗	No	✓	✗	No	✓	?	
Nature's Own	FLO	?	✗	No	?	?	No	?	?	
Oatmeal Goodness	RAL	✗	✓	No	✓	✓	No	✓	✗	dolphins caught
Oro Wheat	MO	✗	✓	No	?	✓	Yes	✗	?	cigarettes
Pepperidge Farm	CPB	✓	✓	No	✓	✓	No	✓	✓	on-site daycare
Sahara	CPC	✗	✓	No	✓	✓	No	✓	✓	
Thomas	CPC	✗	✓	No	✓	✓	No	✓	✓	
Wonder	RAL	✗	✓	No	✓	✓	No	✓	✗	dolphins caught

Company or Product	Abbr.	⚥										ALERT
CANDY & GUM												
3 Musketeers	MARS	?	✓	?	No	?	✗	?	No	?	?	
5th Avenue	HSY	✓	✓	✓	No	?	✓	?	No	✓	✓	
Almond Joy	CADB	✓	✓	✗	No	✓	✓	✓	Yes†	?	✓	
Baby Ruth	RJR	✓	✓	✓	No	✓	?	?	Yes*	✗	✗	cigarettes
Bar None	HSY	✓	✓	✓	No	✓	✓	✓	No	✓	✓	
Bazooka	TOPP	?	✗	✗	No	?	✓	?	No	✓	?	
Big Mouth	TOPP	?	✗	✗	No	?	✓	✓	No	✓	✓	
Big Block	HSY	✓	✓	✓	No	✓	✓	?	No	✓	✓	
Big Red	WWY	?	✓	?	No	?	✗	?	No	?	?	

✓ = Top Rating   ✓̸ = Middle Rating   ✗ = Bottom Rating   ? = Insufficient Information

For a more detailed explanation see key on page 10

CANDY & GUM

Company or Product	Abbr.	💲	♀		✈			No	⚛		❓	✨	ALERT
Bit-O-Honey	NEST	?	?	✓	No	✓	?	No	✓	Yes†	?	✓	infant formula
Bonkers	RJR	✓	✓	✓	No	?	✓	No	?	Yes*	✗	✗	cigarettes
Breathsavers	RJR	✓	✓	✓	No	?	✓	No	?	Yes*	✗	✗	cigarettes
Bubble Yum	RJR	✓	✓	✓	No	?	✓	No	?	Yes*	✗	✗	cigarettes
Bubblicious	WLA	✓	✓	✓	No	✗○	✓	No	✓	Yes●	✓	✓	
Butterfinger	RJR	✓	✓	✓	No	?	✓	No	✓	Yes*	✗	✗	cigarettes
Cadbury	CADB	✓	✗	✓	No	?	✓	No	✓	Yes†	?†	✓	
Caramel	MO	✗	✓	✓	No	✓	✓	No	✓	Yes	✗	✗	cigarettes
Carefree	RJR	✓	✓	✓	No	?	✓	No	?	Yes*	✗	✗	cigarettes
Charleston Chew	RJR	✓	✓	✓	No	?	✓	No	?	Yes*	✗	✗	cigarettes
Chewels	WLA	✓	✓	✓	No	✗○	✓	No	✓	Yes●	✓	✓	
Chiclets	WLA	✓	✓	✓	No	✗○	✓	No	✓	Yes●	✓	✓	

Company or Product	Abbr.	⚥	$	🌐	✈	🐟	🔬	⚛	🏭	🌿	ALERT
Chunky	NEST	?	?	?	No	?	✓	✓	No	Yes†	?	infant formula
Clorets	WLA	✓	✗	✓	No	✗○	✓	✓	No	Yes●	✓	
Confeti	MO	✗	✓	✓	No	?	✓	✗	No	Yes	✗	cigarettes
Dentyne	WLA	✓	✓	✓	No	✗○	✓	✓	No	Yes●	✓	
Doublemint	WWY	?	✓	?	No	?	✗	?	No	No	?	
Extra	WWY	?	✓	?	No	?	✗	?	No	No	?	
Fantastic Foods#	FFI	✗	✗	✗	No	✓	✓	✗	No	No	✗	
Freedent	WWY	?	✓	?	No	?	✗	?	No	No	?	
Freshen-Up	WLA	✓	✓	✓	No	✗○	✓	✓	No	Yes●	✓	
Godiva	CPB	✓	✓	✓	No	✓	✓	✓	No	No	✓	on-site daycare

✓ = Top Rating   ✓ = Middle Rating   ✗ = Bottom Rating   ? = Insufficient Information

For a more detailed explanation see key on page 10

CANDY & GUM

CANDY & GUM

Company or Product	Abbr.	$	♀		✈			⚛			ALERT
Goobers	NEST	?	?	?	No	?	✗	No	Yes†	?	infant formula
Hershey's	HSY	✓	?	✓	No	?	✓	No	No	✓	
Hubba Bubba	WWY	?	?	?	No	?	✗	No	No	?	
Jr. Mints	WLA	✓	✓	✓	No	✗○	✓	No	Yes●	✓	
Juicyfruit	WWY	?	?	✓	No	?	✗	No	No	?	
Kit Kat	HSY	✓	✓	✓	No	?	✓	No	No	✓	
Krackel	HSY	✓	✓	✓	No	?	✓	No	No	✓	
Kraft	MO	✗	✓	✓	No	?	✗	No	Yes	✗	cigarettes
Kudos	MARS	✗	?	✓	No	?	✓	No	No	?	
Licorice Nips	RJR	✓	✓	✓	No	?	?	No	Yes*	✗	cigarettes
Lifesavers	RJR	✓	✓	✓	No	?	?	No	Yes*	✗	cigarettes
Luden's	HSY	✓	✓	✓	No	?	✓	No	No	✓	

Company or Product	Abbr.	💲	♀	✈	?	🐇	⚛	🕊	ALERT
M & M's	MARS	?	?	No	?	✗	?	No	?	
Mars	MARS	?	?	No	- ?	✗	?	No	?	
Mellow	MO	✓	✓	No	?	◐	◐	No	✗	cigarettes
Mentos	WLA	✗	◐	No	✗○	✓	✗	Yes●	✓	
Milky Way	MARS	?	?	No	✓	✗	?	No	✓	
Mounds	CADB	◐	✗	No	✓	◐	◐	Yes†	✓	
Mr. Goodbar	HSY	✓	✓	No	✓	◐	✓	No	✓	
Natura#	NFS	?	?	No	◐	◐	✗	No	?	
Nestle	NEST	?	?	No	?	◐	✗	Yes†	✓	infant formula
Oh Henry!	NEST	?	?	No	?	◐	✗	Yes†	✓	infant formula

✓ = Top Rating   ◐ = Middle Rating   ✗ = Bottom Rating   ? = Insufficient Information

For a more detailed explanation see key on page 10

CANDY & GUM

Company or Product	Abbr.	$	⚥								ALERT
Peter Paul	CADB	✓	✓	✗	No	✓	No	Yes†	?	✓	
Pom Poms	RJR	✓	✓	✓	No	✓	No	Yes*	✗	✗	cigarettes
Pop Rocks	MO	✗	✓	✓	No	✓	No	Yes	?	?	cigarettes
Push Pop	TOPP	?	✗	✗	No	✓	No	No	✓	?	
Raisinets	NEST	✓	?	?	No	✓	No	Yes†	?	✓	infant formula
Reese's	HSY	✓	✓	✓	No	✓	No	No	✓	✓	
Ring Pop	TOPP	?	✗	✗	No	?	No	No	?	?	
Rolo	HSY	✓	✓	✓	No	✓	No	No	?	?	
Skittles	MARS	?	?	?	No	✗	No	No	?	?	
Snickers	MARS	?	?	?	No	✗	No	No	?	?	
Sno-Caps	NEST	?	?	?	No	✓	No	Yes†	✗	✓	infant formula
Solitaires	HSY	✓	✓	✓	No	✓	No	No	✓	✓	

Company or Product	Abbr.	💲	⚥	👥	✈	☢	⚛✂	ALERT
Special Dark	HSY	✓	✓	✓	No	✓	No	✓	
Starburst	MARS	?	?	?	No	?	No	?	
Sticklets	WLA	✓	✓	✗	No	✓	Yes●	✓	
Sugar Babies	WLA	✓	✓	○✗	No	✓	Yes●	✓	
Summit	MARS	?	?	?	No	✗	No	?	
Topps	TOPP	?	✗	?	No	✓	No	?	
Trident	WLA	✓	✓	○✗	No	✓	Yes●	✓	
Twix	MARS	?	?	?	No	✗	No	?	
Twizzler's	HSY	✓	✓	?	No	✓	No	✓	
Wacky Fruit	RJR	✓	?	?	No	?	No	✗	cigarettes

✓ = Top Rating ✓ = Middle Rating ✗ = Bottom Rating ? = Insufficient Information

For a more detailed explanation see key on page 10

CANDY & GUM

Company or Product	Abbr.	$	⚥	✊	✈	🌐	🐇	⚛	👪	ALERT
Whatchamacallit	HSY	✓	✓	?	No	√	✓	No	✓	
Whitman's Chocolates	WH	√	√	√	No	○	✗	No	√	
Winter Fresh	WWY	?	√	?	No	?	✗	No	?	
Wrigley's	WWY	?	√	?	No	?	✗	No	?	
York Peppermint Patties	CADB	√	√	✗	No	√	√	Yes†	?	
CEREAL										
40+ Bran Flakes	K	✓	✓	✓	No	✓	✓	Yes●	✓	
All-Bran	K	✓	✗	✓	No	✓	✓	Yes●	✓	
Alpha-Bits	MO	✗	✓	✓	No	√	✗	Yes	?	cigarettes
Apple Jacks	K	✓	✓	✓	No	✓	✓	Yes●	✓	
Apple Raisin Crisp	K	✓	✓	✓	No	✓	✓	Yes●	✓	
Arrowhead Mills#	AM	?	√	√	No	√	?	No	√	

Company or Product	Abbr.	1	2	3	4	5	6	7	8	9	10	ALERT
Barbara's Bakery#	BARB	?	✓	✓	No	✓	✓	✓(mid)	No	✓	✗	
Boo Berry	GIS	✓+	✓	✓	No	✓	✓	✓	No	✓	✓	
Bran Buds	K	✓	✓	?	No	?	✓	✓	Yes●	✓(mid)	✓	
Buc Wheats	GIS	✓+	✓	✓	No	✓	✓	✓	No	✓(mid)	✓	
Cap'n Crunch	OAT	✓(mid)	?	✓	No	✓(mid)	✓	✓	No	✓	✓	
Carnation	NEST	?	?	✓	No	✓(mid)	✓(mid)	✗	Yes†	?	✓	infant formula
Cheerios	GIS	✓+	?	✓	No	✓	✓	✓	No	✓(mid)	✓	
Chex	RAL	✗	✗	✗	No	✓	✓	✓(mid)	No	✓(mid)	✗	dolphins caught
Cinnamon Toast Crunch	GIS	✓+	✓	✓	No	✓	✓	✓	No	✓(mid)	✓	
Clusters	GIS	✓+	✓(mid)	✓	No	✓	✓	✓(mid)	No	✓(mid)	✓	

✓ = Top Rating   ✓(mid) = Middle Rating   ✗ = Bottom Rating   ? = Insufficient Information

For a more detailed explanation see key on page 10

CEREAL

Company or Product	Abbr.	💲	⚥	〰	✈	🐰	🖐	⚛	🤡	🐄	❂	ALERT
Cocoa Krispies	K	✔	✔	✔	No	?	✔	✔	No	Yes●	✔	✔	
Cocoa Puffs	GIS	✔+	✔	✔	No	✔	✔	✔	No	No	✔	✔	
Cookie Crisp	RAL	✖	✔	✖	No	✔	✔	✔	No	No	✔	✖	dolphins caught
Corn Pops	K	✔	✔	✔	No	?	✔	✔	No	Yes●	✔	✔	
Corn Flakes	K	✔	✔	✔	No	?	✔	✔	No	Yes●	✔	✔	
Count Chocula	GIS	✔+	✔	✔	No	?	✔	✔	No	No	✔	✔	
Cracklin' Oat Bran	K	✔	✔	✔	No	?	✔	✔	No	Yes●	✔	✔	
Cream of Wheat	RJR	✔	✔	✖	No	?	?	✔	No	Yes✱	✖	✖	cigarettes
Cremerie Triple Cream	MO	✖	✔	✔	No	?	?	✔	No	Yes	✖	?	cigarettes
Crispix	K	✔	✔	✔	No	?	?	✔	No	Yes●	✔	✔	
Crispy Critters	MO	✖	✔	✔	No	?	?	✔	No	Yes	✖	?	cigarettes
Croonchy Stars	MO	✖	✔	✔	No	?	?	✔	No	Yes	✖	?	cigarettes

Company or Product	Abbr.	$	♀	✊	✈	🐇	🌍	☢	🏠	ℹ	ALERT
Crunchberry	OAT	✓	✓	✓	No	✓	✓	No	✓	✓	
Deer Valley Farm#	DVF	✗	✓	✗	No	✓	?	No	✓	✗	
Eden#	EDEN	✗	✗	✗	No	✓	✓	No	✗	✗	
El Molino#	AMH	?	✓	✓	No	?	✗	No	?	✗	
Evon's#	JSAN	?	?	✗	No	✓	✓	No	✓	✓	
Farina	GMP	?	?	?	?	?	✗	?	Yes+	?	dolphins caught
Franken Berry	GIS	✓+	✓	✓	No	✓	✓	No	✓	✓	
Frosted Flakes	K	✓	✓	✓	No	?	✓	No	Yes●	✓	
Frosted Rice Krinkles	MO	✗	✓	✓	No	?	✓	No	Yes	?	cigarettes
Froot Loops	K	✓	✓	✓	No	?	✓	No	Yes●	✓	

✓ = Top Rating ✓ = Middle Rating ✗ = Bottom Rating ? = Insufficient Information
For a more detailed explanation see key on page 10

Page 81

CEREAL

Company or Product	Abbr.	💲	⚥					⚛				ALERT
Fruit & Fibre	MO	✗	✓	✓	No	?	✓	No	Yes	✗	?	cigarettes
Fruitful Bran	K	✓	✓	✓	No	?	✓	No	Yes●	✓	✓	
General Foods	MO	✗	✓	✓	No	?	✓	No	Yes	✗	?	cigarettes
General Mills	GIS	✓+	✓	✓	No	?	✓	No	No	✓	✓	
Golden Crisp	MO	✗	✓	✓	No	?	✓	No	Yes	✗	?	cigarettes
Golden Grahams	GIS	✓+	✓	✓	No	?	✓	No	No	✓	✓	
Grape-Nuts	MO	✗	✓	✓	No	?	✓	No	Yes	✗	?	cigarettes
Health Valley Nat. Foods#	HVAL	?	✓	✓	No	?	?	No	No	✓	✗	
Honey Smacks	K	✓	✓	✓	No	?	✓	No	Yes●	✓	✓	
Honey Nut Crunch	MO	✗	✓	✓	No	?	✓	No	Yes	✗	?	cigarettes
Honeycomb	MO	✗	✓	✓	No	?	✓	No	Yes	✗	?	cigarettes
Horizon	MO	✗	✓	✓	No	?	✓	No	Yes	✗	?	cigarettes

Company or Product	Abbr.	💲	♀	🧑	🪖	❓	🐇	🌿	⚛	👪	✿	ALERT
Just Right	K	✔	✔	✔	No	?	✔	✔	No	✔	✔	
Kellogg's	K	✔	✔	✔	No	?	✔	✔	Yes●	✔	✔	
Kix	GIS	✔+	✔	✔	No	🗸	🗸	✔	No	🗸	✔	
Kretschmer Wheat Germ	OAT	✔	✔	✔	No	🗸	✔	✔	No	✔	✔	
Life	OAT	✔	✔	✔	No	🗸	✔	✔	No	🗸	✔	
Lucky Charms	GIS	✔+	✔	✔	No	✔	🗸	✔	No	✔	✔	
Mayo Oatmeal	AHP	✘	🗸	✘	No	✔(*)	✔	🗸	Yes*	🗸	✘	infant formula
Mother's Rolled Oats	OAT	✔	✔	✔	No	?	🗸	✔	No	✔	✔	
Mueslix	K	✔	✔	✔	No	?	✔	✔	Yes●	✔	✔	
Nabisco Fruit Wheats	RJR	✔	🗸	🗸	No	?	?	🗸	Yes*	✘	✘	cigarettes

✔ = Top Rating   🗸 = Middle Rating   ✘ = Bottom Rating   ? = Insufficient Information

For a more detailed explanation see key on page 10

Page 83

Company or Product	Abbr.	$	[icon]	[airplane/tree]	[animal]	[hand]	[chess]	⚛	[people]	[skull]	ALERT
Nabisco Raisin Bran	RJR	✓	✓	No	?	✓	?	No	Yes*	✗	cigarettes
Nut & Honey Crunch	K	✓	✓	No	?	✓	?	No	Yes●	✓	
Nutri-Grain	K	✓	✓	No	?	✓	?	No	Yes●	✓	
Oatmeal Raisin Crisp	GIS	✓+	✓	No	✓	✓	✓	No	No	✓	
Oh's	OAT	✓	✓	No	✓	✓	✓	No	No	✓	
Pebbles	MO	✗	✓	No	?	✓	✓	No	Yes	?	cigarettes
Post	MO	✗	✓	No	?	✓	✓	No	Yes	?	cigarettes
Post Grape Nuts	MO	✗	✓	No	?	✓	✓	No	Yes	?	cigarettes
Post Raisin Bran	MO	✗	✓	No	?	✓	✓	No	Yes●	?	cigarettes
Product 19	K	✓	✓	No	?	✓	✓	No	Yes●	✓	
Quaker	OAT	✓	✓	No	?	✓	✓	No	No	✓	
Raisin Bran	MO	✗	✓	No	?	✓	✓	No	Yes	?	cigarettes

CEREAL

Company or Product	Abbr.	💲	⚥	🗺	✍	–	🦅	⚛	🌸	💎	ALERT
Raisin Nut Bran	GIS	✔+	✓	✓	✓	No	✓	No	✓	✓	
Ralston	RAL	✗	✓	✗	✓	No	✓	No	✗	✗	dolphins caught
Rice Krispies	K	✓	✓	✓	✓	No	?	Yes●	✓	✓	
Rusket	LOMA	?	✓	✓	✓	No	✓	No	✓	✗	
S.W. Graham	K	✓	✓	✓	✓	No	?	Yes●	✓	✓	
Shredded Wheat	RJR	✓	✓	✓	?	No	?	Yes*	✗	✗	cigarettes
Smurf Magic Berries	MO	✗	✓	✓	✓	No	?	Yes	✗	?	cigarettes
Special K	K	✓	✓	✓	✓	No	?	Yes●	✓	✓	cigarettes
Spoon Size	RJR	✓	✓	✓	?	No	?	Yes*	✗	✗	cigarettes
Super Golden Crisp	MO	✗	✓	✓	✓	No	✓	Yes	✗	?	cigarettes

✔ = Top Rating   ✓ = Middle Rating   ✗ = Bottom Rating   ? = Insufficient Information

For a more detailed explanation see key on page 10

CEREAL

CEREAL

Company or Product	Abbr.	$	⚥	◨	✈	🐄	✊	👤	☢	🕊	?	ALERT
Toasties	MO	✗	✓	✓	No	?	✓	✓	No	✗	?	cigarettes
Total	GIS	✓+	✓	✓	No	✓	✓	✓	No	✓	✓	
Treat-Pak	MO	✗	✓	✓	No	?	✓	✓	No	✗	?	cigarettes
Trix	GIS	✓+	✓	✓	No	?	✓	✓	No	✓	✓	
Wheatena	AHP	✗	✗	✓	No	✓(*)	✓	✓	No	✓	✗	infant formula
Wheaties	GIS	✓+	✓	✓	No	?	✓	✓	No	✓	✓	
CHEESE												
21st Century Foods#	TFC	✗	✓	✓	No	✓	✓	✓	No	✓	✓	
Adler	CPC	✗	✓	✓	No	✓	✓	✓	No	✓	✓	
Armour	CAG	?	✓	?	No	?	✗	?	?	✓	?	OSHA fines
Beatrice	BTC	✓+	✓	?	No	✓	✓	✓	No	✓	✓	
Breakstone's	MO	✗	✗	✓	No	?	✓	✓	Yes	✗	?	cigarettes

Company or Product	Abbr.	$	♀	⚒	✈	🏃	⚛	🐾	💀	☠	ALERT
Breyers	MO	✗	✓	?	No	?	✓	No	Yes	✗	?	cigarettes
Butterfly	BTC	✓+	✓	?	No	?	✓	No	No	✓	?	
Casino	MO	✗	✓	?	No	?	✓	No	Yes	✗	?	cigarettes
Cheese Whip	MO	✗	✓	?	No	?	✓	No	Yes	✗	?	cigarettes
Churny	MO	✗	✓	?	No	?	✓	No	Yes	✗	?	cigarettes
Coon	MO	✗	✓	?	No	?	✓	No	Yes	✗	?	cigarettes
County Line	BTC	✓+	✓	?	No	?	✓	No	No	✓	?	
Courtland Star	UFC	✓	✓	✗	No	✓	✓	No	No	?	?	
Cracker Barrel	MO	✗	✓	?	No	?	✓	No	Yes	✗	?	cigarettes
Cream Chie#	TFC	✗	✓	✓	No	✓	?	No	No	✓	✓	

✔ = Top Rating ✓ = Middle Rating ✗ = Bottom Rating ? = Insufficient Information
For a more detailed explanation see key on page 10

Page 87

CHEESE

Company or Product	Abbr.	💲	⚥	✈	✊	⚛	♻	👪	🕊	ALERT
Dean	DF	?	✗	?	No	✓	✗	No	No	?	✗	
Fisher	BN	✗	✓	✓	No	✓	✓	No	Yes●	✓	✓	
Ile de France	UFC	✓	✓	✗	No	✓	?	No	No	?	?	
Jersey Maid	MO	✗	✓	✓	No	✓	✓	No	Yes	✗	?	cigarettes
Knudsen	MO	✗	✓	✓	No	✓	✓	No	Yes	✗	?	cigarettes
La Belle France	UFC	✓	✓	✓	No	✓	?	No	No	?	?	
Light n' Lively	MO	✗	✓	✓	No	✓	?	No	Yes	✓	?	cigarettes
Lily Lake	BTC	✓+	✓	✓	No	✓	?	No	No	✓	?	
Lite-line	BN	✗	✓	✓	No	✓	✓	No	Yes●	✓	✓	
Lorraine	UFC	✓	✓	✓	No	✓	?	No	No	?	?	
Maman Luise	MO	✗	✓	✓	No	✓	✓	No	Yes	✗	?	cigarettes
Paul Jean Barnett	MO	✗	✓	✓	No	✓	✓	No	Yes	✗	?	cigarettes

Company or Product	Abbr	$	⚥	✈	⋯	▪	⚛	▫	🐇	⊕	ALERT
Phila. Cream Cheese	MO	✗	✔	No	?	✔	No	✔	✗	?	cigarettes
Polly-O	MO	✗	✔	No	?	✔	Yes	✔	✗	?	cigarettes
Red Rooster	MO	✗	✔	No	?	✔	No	✔	✗	?	cigarettes
Sealtest	MO	✗	✔	No	?	✔	Yes	✔	✗	?	cigarettes
Select-A-Size	MO	✗	✔	No	?	✔	No	✔	✗	?	cigarettes
Temp Tee	MO	✗	✔	No	?	✔	Yes	✔	✗	?	cigarettes
Tillamook Cheese	TILA	✗	✔	No	✔	✔	No	?	✗	✗	
Tofu Cream Chie#	TFC	✗	✔	No	✔	✔	No	?	✔	✔	
Velveeta	MO	✗	✔	No	?	✔	No	✔	✗	?	cigarettes
Weight Watchers	HNZ	✔	✔	No	✔	✗	No	✔	✔	✔	dolphins caught

✔ = Top Rating ✓ = Middle Rating ✗ = Bottom Rating ? = Insufficient Information

For a more detailed explanation see key on page 10

CHEESE

Company or Product	Abbr.	💲♀	⚒	✈	🌍	✊	⚛	🐾	ALERT
Yorkshire Farm	UB	✓	✓	No	✓	✗	No	✓	labor disputes
COCOA									
Carnation	NEST	?	?	No	✓	✗	Yes†	?	infant formula
Hershey	HSY	✓	✓	No	✓	✓	No	✓	
Nestle	NEST	?	?	No	✓	✗	Yes†	✓	infant formula
Quik	NEST	?	?	No	✓	✗	Yes†	✓	infant formula
Swiss Miss	BTC	✓+	✓	No	✓	?	No	?	
Weight Watchers	HNZ	✓	✓	No	✓	✓	Yes	✓	dolphins caught
COFFEE									
Brava	NEST	?	?	No	✓	✗	Yes†	✓	infant formula
Brim	MO	✗	✓	No	✓	✓	Yes	✗	cigarettes
Bustelo	ALP	?	?	No	✗	?	Yes†	?	

Company or Product	Abbr.	💲	♀	◆	✈	◆	◆	⚛	◆	◆	ALERT
Eight O'Clock	GAP	?	✓	∨	No	✓	∨	No	∨	∨	refuses cans
Folgers	PG	✓	✓	✓	No	✓(*)	✓	No	∨	✓	disposable diapers
General Foods Int'l Cof.	MO	✗	✓	✓	No	?	∨	No	✗	?	cigarettes
Gevalia	MO	✗	✓	✓	No	?	∨	No	✗	?	cigarettes
Hag	MO	✗	✓	✓	No	?	∨	No	✗	?	cigarettes
High Point	PG	✓	✓	✓	No	✓(*)	✓	No	∨	∨	disposable diapers
Kava	BN	✗	✓	∨	No	✓	∨	Yes●	∨	∨	
Lyons	ALP	?	?	?	No	?	✗	Yes†	?	?	
Martinson	ALP	?	?	?	No	?	✗	Yes†	?	?	
Master Blend	MO	✗	✓	✓	No	?	∨	No	✗	?	cigarettes

✓ = Top Rating ∨ = Middle Rating ✗ = Bottom Rating ? = Insufficient Information

For a more detailed explanation see key on page 10

COFFEE

Company or Product	Abbr.	💲	⚥	✈	🐇	🗑	🏠	⚛	🕊	♲	ALERT
Maxim	MO	✗	✓	No	?	✓	✓	Yes	✗	?	cigarettes
Maxwell House	MO	✗	✓	No	?	✓	✓	Yes	✗	?	cigarettes
Medaglia D'Oro	ALP	?	?	No	?	✗	?	Yes†	?	?	
Nescafe	NEST	?	?	No	?	✗	✗	Yes†	?	✓	infant formula
Postum	MO	✗	✓	No	?	✓	✓	Yes	✗	?	cigarettes
Sanka	MO	✗	✓	No	?	✓	✓	Yes	✗	?	cigarettes
Savarin	ALP	?	?	No	?	✗	✓	Yes†	?	?	
Taster's Choice	NEST	?	?	No	✓	✗	✗	Yes†	?	✓	infant formula
Tio Sancho	MCRK	✓+	✗	No	✓	✓	?	No	✓	✗	
Yuban	MO	✗	✓	No	?	✓	✓	Yes	✗	?	cigarettes
CONDIMENTS & SAUCES											
A-1	RJR	✓	✓	No	?	✓	?	Yes*	✗	✗	cigarettes

Company or Product	Abbr.	💲	⚥	✈	⚒	🐁	⚛	🐾	🌿	ALERT
Annie's Farmhouse#	CHER	?	✗	No	✓	✓	No	✓	?	
Arrowhead Mills#	AM	?	✓	No	?	✓	No	✓	✓	
Aunt Millie's	BN	✗	✓	No	✓	✓	No	Yes●	✓	
Bennett's	BN	✗	✓	No	✓	✓	No	Yes●	✓	
Bull's-Eye	MO	✗	✗	No	?	✓	No	Yes	?	cigarettes
Cherry Hill#	CHER	?	✓	No	✓	✓	No	No	?	
Classic O	BN	✗	✓	No	?	✓	No	Yes●	✓	
Claussen	MO	✗	✓	No	?	✓	No	Yes	?	cigarettes
Contadina	NEST	?	?	No	✗	✗	No	Yes†	✓	infant formula
Crosse & Blackwell	NEST	?	?	No	✗	✗	No	Yes†	?	infant formula

✓ = Top Rating   ✓ = Middle Rating   ✗ = Bottom Rating   ? = Insufficient Information
For a more detailed explanation see key on page 10

CONDIMENTS & SAUCES

CONDIMENTS & SAUCES

Company or Product	Abbr.	💲	⚥	✊	✈	⚙	🏃	⚛	🌲	🐇	ALERT
Del Monte	RJR	✓	✓	✓	No	?	✓	No	Yes*	✗	cigarettes
Eden#	EDEN	✗	✗	✗	No	✓	✓	No	No	✗	
Eggo	K	✓	✓	✓	No	?	✓	No	Yes●	✓	
El Molino	BN	✗	✓	✓	No	✓	✓	No	Yes●	✓	
Emperor's Kitchen	GES	?	✓	✓	No	✓	✗	No	No	✗	
Fantastic Foods#	FFI	?	✓	✗	No	✓	✗	No	No	✗	
Filomena's Marinara#	CHER	?	✗	✗	No	?	✓	No	No	?	
Grey Poupon Dijon	RJR	✓	✓	✓	No	?	✓	No	Yes*	✗	cigarettes
Gulden's Mustard	AHP	✗	✗	✗	No	✓(*)	✓	No	Yes*	✗	infant formula
Health Valley Nat. Foods#	HVAL	?	✓	✗	No	✓	✓	No	Yes	✗	
Heinz	HNZ	✓	✓	✓	No	?	✓	No	Yes	✓	dolphins caught
Hunt's	BTC	✓+	✓	?	No	?	✓	No	No	✓	

Company or Product	Abbr.	⊕	⚥	✊	🐇	✈	⚛	🐾	◊	ALERT
Joe's#	DVF	✗	✓	?	✓	No	No	✓	✗	
KC Masterpiece	CLX	✓	✓	✓	✓*	No	No	✓	✓	
Kraft	MO	✗	✓	✓	?	No	Yes	✗	?	cigarettes
Kraft Horseradish	MO	✗	✓	✓	?	No	Yes	✗	?	cigarettes
La Croix	CPB	✓	✗	✓	?	No	No	✓	✓	on-site daycare
Lawry's	UN	✗	✓	✗	✓*	No	Yes†	?	?	
Le Gout	K	✓	✗	✓	?	No	Yes●	✓	✓	
Lifetone International*	LFTI	?	✗	✗	✓	No	No	?	?	
Little Pancho	BN	✗	✓	✓	✓	No	Yes●	✓	✓	
Magic Touch	BTC	✓+	?	?	?	No	No	✓	✓	

✓ = Top Rating   √ = Middle Rating   ✗ = Bottom Rating   ? = Insufficient Information
For a more detailed explanation see key on page 10

Page 95

CONDIMENTS & SAUCES

CONDIMENTS & SAUCES

Company or Product	Abbr.	💲	♀	🧑‍🤝‍🧑	🔥	🤝	✊	⚛	🌍	🐾	ALERT
Makin' Cajun	MO	✗	✓	✓	No	?	✓	No	Yes	✗	cigarettes
Manwich	BTC	✓+	✓	?	No	?	✓	No	No	✓	
Mayacamas#	MAYA	?	?	?	No	✓	✓	No	No	✗	
McCormick	MCRK	✓+	✓	?	No	✓	?	No	No	✗	
Miguel's Salsa#	CHER	?	✓	✗	No	✓	✓	No	No	?	
Miso Master#	GES	?	✓	✓	No	✓	✗	No	No	✗	
Natura#	NFS	?	?	?	No	✓	✗	No	No	?	
Newman's Own	NEWO	✓+	✓	✗	No	✓	✓	No	No	✓	profit to charity
Old Monk#	DFAM	?	?	✓	No	✓	✓	No	No	✓	
Open Pit	CPB	✓	✓	✓	No	✓	✓	No	No	✓	on-site daycare
Pacific Gardens#	ACOP	?	✓	✗	No	✓	✓	No	No	✓	
Prego	CPB	✓	✓	✓	No	✓	✓	No	No	✓	on-site daycare

Company or Product	Abbr.	$	♀	✊	✈	🐭	⚒	⚛	🌍	👪	ALERT
Progresso	WH	✓	✓	✓	No	✓○	✗	No	?	✓	
Ragu	UN	✗	✓	✓	No	✓*	✗	Yes†	?	?	
San-J International#	SANJ	?	✓	✓	No	✓	✗	No	✓	✗	
Smokehouse	HRL	✓	✗	✗	No	✓	✗	No	✓	✗	labor disputes
Sterling#	DFAM	?	✓	?	No	✓	✗	No	✓	✓	
Sweet Cloud#	GES	?	✓	?	No	✓	✗	No	✓	✗	
Thick 'N Spicy	MO	✗	✓	✓	No	?	✓	Yes	✗	?	cigarettes
Vlasic	CPB	✓	✓	✓	No	?	✗	No	✓	✓	on-site daycare
Wizard	AHP	✗	✓	✓	No	✓(*)	✓	Yes*	✓	✗	infant formula
Yorkshire Farm	UB	✓	✓	✓	No	✓	✗	No	?	✓	labor disputes

✓ = Top Rating ✓ = Middle Rating ✗ = Bottom Rating ? = Insufficient Information	**Page 97**

For a more detailed explanation see key on page 10

CONDIMENTS & SAUCES

Company or Product	Abbr.	💲	♀	🤝	🎖	🏃	🌍	⚛	🐇	ALERT
CRACKERS & BREAD PRODUCTS										
Ann Page	GAP	?	✓	✓	No	✓	✓	No	✓	refuses cans
Arnold	CPC	✗	✓	✓	No	✓	✓	No	✓	
Barbara's Bakery#	BARB	?	✓	✓	No	✓	?	No	✓	
Better Cheddars	RJR	✓	✓	✓	No	?	?	Yes*	✗	cigarettes
Chicken Helper	GIS	✓+	✓	✓	No	✓	✓	No	✗	
Classic	RJR	✓	✓	✓	No	?	?	Yes*	✗	cigarettes
Colonial	BUD	✓+	✓	✓	No	✓	✓	No	✓	
Corn Flake Crumbs	K	✓	✓	✓	No	✓	✓	Yes●	✓	
Devonsheer	CPC	✗	✓	✓	No	✓	✓	No	✓	
El Molino#	AMH	?	?	✓	No	✗	?	No	?	
Entenmann's	MO	✗	✓	✓	No	✓	?	Yes	✗	cigarettes

Company or Product	Abbr.	💲	⚥	✊	🐦	?	⚛	🐾	🕊	ALERT
Evon's #	JSAN	?	✔	✗	No	?	✔	No	✔	
Falcon Trading #	FALC	?	✔	✗	No	✔	✔	No	✓	
Fantastic Foods #	FFI	?	✔	✗	No	✗	✔	No	✗	
Friehofer's	MO	✗	✔	✔	No	✔	?	Yes	?	cigarettes
General Foods	MO	✗	✔	✔	No	✔	✗	Yes	?	cigarettes
Gold Label	BUD	✔+	✔	✔	No	✔	✔	No	✓	
Hamburger Helper	GIS	✔+	✔	✔	No	✔	✔	No	✗	
Health Valley Nat. Foods #	HVAL	?	✔	✔	No	?	✔	No	✗	
Keebler	UBH	?	?	?	No	?	?	No	✗	
Kellogg's	K	✔	✔	✔	No	✔	✔	Yes●	✔	

✔ = Top Rating   ✓ = Middle Rating   ✗ = Bottom Rating   ? = Insufficient Information

For a more detailed explanation see key on page 10

CRACKERS & BREAD PRODUCTS

CRACKERS & BREAD PRODUCTS

Company or Product	Abbr.	💲	♀	⬛	✈	🐇	🔬	⚛	🕊	🌐	ALERT
Kilpatrick's	BUD	✓+	✓	✓	No	✓	✓	No	No	✓	
Lifetone International#	LFTI	?	✗	✗	No	✓	✓	No	No	?	
Minute Rice	MO	✗	✓	✓	No	?	✓	No	Yes	✗	cigarettes
Mrs. Dash	ACV	?	?	?	No	✗	?	No	No	?	
Nabisco	RJR	✓	✓	✓	No	?	✓	No	Yes*	✗	cigarettes
Oro Wheat	MO	✗	✓	✓	No	✓	✓	No	Yes	?	cigarettes
Oven Fry	MO	✗	✓	✓	No	✓	✓	No	Yes	?	cigarettes
Pepperidge Farm	CPB	✓	✓	✓	No	✓	✓	No	No	✓	on-site daycare
Premium	RJR	✓	✓	?	No	?	?	No	Yes*	✗	cigarettes
Progresso	WH	✓	✓	✓	No	✓○	✗	No	No	✓	
Quick Rise	GIS	✓+	✓	✓	No	✓	✓	No	No	✓	
Ritz	RJR	✓	✓	✓	No	?	?	No	Yes*	✗	cigarettes

Company or Product	Abbr.	$	♀								ALERT
Ry Krisp	RAL	✖	✓	✖	No	✓	✓	No	✓	✖	dolphins caught
San-J International#	SANJ	?	✓	✓	No	✓	✓	No	✓	✖	
Shake 'n Bake	MO	✖	✓	✓	No	?	✓	Yes	✖	?	cigarettes
Sociables	RJR	✓	✓	✓	No	?	?	Yes*	✖	✖	cigarettes
Stove Top	MO	✖	✓	✓	No	?	✓	Yes	✖	?	cigarettes
Sunflower	RJR	✓	✓	✓	No	?	?	Yes*	✖	✖	cigarettes
Sunshine	AMB	✓	✖	✓	No	✓	?	Yes	?	✖	cigarettes
The Huntley & Palmer	RJR	✓	✓	✓	No	?	?	Yes*	✖	✖	cigarettes
Triscuit	RJR	✓	✓	✓	No	?	?	Yes*	✖	✖	cigarettes
Tuna Helper	GIS	✓+	✓	✓	No	✓	✓	No	✓	✓	

✓ = Top Rating ✓ = Middle Rating ✖ = Bottom Rating ? = Insufficient Information	Page 101

For a more detailed explanation see key on page 10

CRACKERS & BREAD PRODUCTS

Company or Product	Abbr.	$	♀	💧	✈	🏃	✎	⚛	🌍	♻	🐰	ALERT
Uneeda	RJR	✓	✓	✓	No	?	✓	No	Yes*	✗	✗	cigarettes
Waverly	RJR	✓	✓	✓	No	?	✓	No	Yes*	✗	✗	cigarettes
Wheat Thins	RJR	✓	✓	✓	No	?	✓	No	Yes*	✗	✗	cigarettes
Wheatsworth	RJR.	✓	✓	✓	No	?	✓	No	Yes*	✗	✗	cigarettes

DEODORANTS & FRAGRANCES

Company or Product	Abbr.	$	♀	💧	✈	🏃	✎	⚛	🌍	♻	🐰	ALERT
Arrid Extra Dry	CAR	?	✗	?	No	?	✓	No	No	✗○	?	
Aubrey Organics#	AUB	?	✓	✓	No	✓	✓	No	No	✓	✓	
Aura Cacia#	AURA	?	✓	✓	No	✓	✓	No	No	✓	✓	
Avon	AVP	✓	✓	✓	No	✓	✓	No	No	✓	✓	
Ban	BMY	✓	✗	✓	No	?	✓	No	Yes*	✓(*)	✗○	✗	infant formula
Brawn	CAR	?	✗	?	No	?	✗	No	No	✓	?	
Brut 33	FAB	?	✗	?	No	?	✗	No	No	?	?	

Company or Product	Abbr.									ALERT
Dry Idea	GS	◇	◇	No	✓	✗	No		✓	
FDS	ACV	?	?	No	?	✗	No	?	?	
Faberge	FAB	?	?	No	?	✗	No	?		
Foot Guard	GS	◇	◇	No	✓	✗	Yes●	✓	✓	
Footwork	GS	◇	✓	No	✓	✗	Yes●	✓	✓	
Gillette	GS	◇	✓	No	✓	✗	Yes●	✓	✓	
HI & DRI	REVL	?	?	No	◇	✓	Yes●	◇	◇	
Lady's Choice	ACY	◇	?	No	◇	✗○	Yes*	✗	◇	makes pesticides
Mill Creek	CARM	?	?	No	✓	✓	Yes	◇	◇	
Mitchum	REVL	?	?	No	?	✓	Yes●	◇	◇	

✓ = Top Rating   ◇ = Middle Rating   ✗ = Bottom Rating   ? = Insufficient Information

For a more detailed explanation see key on page 10

DEODORANTS & FRAGRANCES

Company or Product	Abbr.	$	♀	✊	✈	🐰	🌐	⚛	👪	🕊	ALERT
Mum	BMY	✓	✓	✓	No	✓(*)	✓	✓	No	Yes*	✗	infant formula
Old Spice	ACY	✓	?	?	No	✗○	✓	✗	No	Yes*	✓	makes pesticides
Orjene Nat. Cosmetics#	ORJ	?	?	✓	No	✓	✓	✗	No	No	✗	
Paul Penders#	PP	?	?	✗	No	✗	✓	✗	No	No	✓	
Right Guard	GS	✓	✓	✓	No	✓(*)	✓	✓	No	Yes●	✓	
Secret	PG	✓	✓	✓	No	✓(*)	✓	✓	No	Yes	✓	disposable diapers
Shower to Shower	JNJ	✓	✓	✓	No	✓(*)	✓	✓	No	Yes*	✓	
Shulton	ACY	✓	?	?	No	✗○	✓	✗	No	Yes*	✗	makes pesticides
So Dry	ACY	✓	?	?	No	✗○	✓	✗	No	Yes*	✓	makes pesticides
Soft & Dri	GS	✓	✓	✓	No	✓(*)	✓	✓	No	Yes●	✓	
Sure	PG	✓	✓	✓	No	✓	✓	✓	No	Yes	✓	disposable diapers

Company or Product	Abbr.	$	♀				⚛				ALERT
Tickle	BMY	✓	✓	No	✓(*)	✓	No	Yes*	?	✗	infant formula
Tom's of Maine#	TOM	✓+	✗	No	✓(*)	✓	No	No	✓	✓	
Trinity	GS	✓	✓	No	✗	✓	No	Yes●	✓	✓	
Ultra Ban	BMY	✓	✓	No	✓(*)	✓	No	Yes*	?	✗	infant formula
DESSERTS											
Bakers	MO	✗	✓	No	?	✓	No	Yes	✗	?	cigarettes
Bird's	MO	✗	✓	No	?	✓	No	Yes	✗	?	cigarettes
Bosco	BN	✗	✓	No	✓	✓	No	Yes●	✓	✓	
Campfire	BN	✗	✓	No	✓	✓	No	Yes●	✓	✓	
Chambourcy	NEST	?	?	No	?	✗	No	Yes†	?	✓	infant formula

✓ = Top Rating   ✓ = Middle Rating   ✗ = Bottom Rating   ? = Insufficient Information

For a more detailed explanation see key on page 10

DESSERTS

Company or Product	Abbr.	💲	♀	✊	✈	♻	☢	🌍	ALERT
Cool Whip	MO	✗	✓	✓	No	✓	No	?	cigarettes
Cover Farms	MO	✗	✓	✓	No	✓	No	?	cigarettes
D-Zerta	MO	✗	✓	✓	No	✓	No	?	cigarettes
Dream Whip	MO	✗	✓	✓	No	✓	No	?	cigarettes
Dutch Maid	K	✓	✓	✓	No	✓	Yes●	✓	
Easy As Pie	K	✓	✓	✓	No	✓	Yes●	✓	
General Foods	MO	✗	✓	✓	No	✓	No	?	cigarettes
Hershey	HSY	✓	✓	✓	No	✓	No	✓	
Homestyle#	HOME	?	✗	✓	No	?	No	?	
Hunt's Snack Pack	BTC	✓+	✓	✓	No	?	No	✓	
Jell-O	MO	✗	✓	✓	No	✓	Yes	✓	cigarettes
La Creme	WH	✓	✓	✓	No	✓	No.	✓	

Company or Product	Abbr.	$	O+					⚛				ALERT
Le Gout	K	✔	✔	No	?	✔	✔	No	Yes●	✔	✔	
Magic Shell	SJM	✓	✗	No	?	✓	✓	No	No	✔	✗	
Minute Tapioca	MO	✗	✔	No	?	✓	✓	No	Yes	✗	?	cigarettes
Mrs. Smith's	K	✔	✔	No	?	✔	✓	No	Yes●	✔	✔	
My★T★Fine	RJR	✔	✓	No	?	?	?	No	Yes*	✗	✗	cigarettes
Nabisco	RJR	✔	✓	No	✔	?	?	No	Yes*	✗	✗	cigarettes
Natura#	NFS	?	?	No	✔	?	✗	No	No	✓	?	
Nestle	NEST	?	?	No	?	✗	✗	No	Yes†	?	✔	infant formula
Pillsbury	GMP	?	?	?	?	✓	?	?	Yes†	?	?	dolphins caught
Reddi-Wip	BTC	✔+	✓	No	?	✓	✓	No	No	✓	✓	

✔ = Top Rating   ✓ = Middle Rating   ✗ = Bottom Rating   ? = Insufficient Information

For a more detailed explanation see key on page 10

DESSERTS

Company or Product	Abbr.	💲	⚥	✊	✈	🐇	👥	⚛	👨‍👩‍👧	🐢	🐾	ALERT
Royal	RJR	✓	✓	✓	No	?	✓	No	Yes*	✗	✗	cigarettes
Smucker's	SJM	✓	?	✗	No	?	✓	No	No	✓	✗	
TastyKake	TBC	✓+	✓	✗	No	?	✓	No	No	✓	✓	
Thank You Brand	CBI	✓+	✓	?	No	?	✓	No	?	✓	✓	

FIRST AID

Company or Product	Abbr.	💲	⚥	✊	✈	🐇	👥	⚛	👨‍👩‍👧	🐢	🐾	ALERT
Athleticare	JNJ	✓	✓	✓	No	✓(*)	✓	No	Yes*	✓	✓	
Bactine	MILS	?	?	✓	No	✗○	?	No	Yes†	?	✗	
Band Aid	JNJ	✓	✓	✓	No	✓(*)	✓	No	Yes*	✓	✓	
Campho-Phenique	EK	✓	✓	✓	Yes	✓(*)	✓	No	No	✓	✓	
Cortaid	UPJ	✓	✓	✓	No	✗○	✓	No	Yes●	✓	✓	
Curad	CL	✓+	✓	✓	No	✓*	✓	No	Yes*	✓	✓	
Curity	CL	✓+	✓	✓	No	✓*	✓	No	Yes*	✓	✓	

Company or Product	Abbr.	$									ALERT
Johnson & Johnson	JNJ	(✓)	✓	No	✓	✓(*)	No	Yes*	✓	✓	
Metaphen	ABT	✗	(✓)	?	✓	✗ ○	No	Yes●	(✓)	✓	infant formula
Solarcaine	SGP	(✓)	(✓)	(✓)	✓	✓(*) ○	No	Yes●	(✓)	(✓)	
Sterri-Strip	MMM	(✓)	✓	✓	✓	✓*	No·	Yes·	✓	✓	
Tindetin	SGP	(✓)	(✓)	(✓)	✓	✓(*)	No	Yes●	(✓)	(✓)	
FISH, CANNED											
Bumble Bee	GMP	?	?	?	?	?	?	Yes†	(✓)	✓	dolphins caught
Carnation	NEST	?	?	?	✗	✓	No	Yes†	?	✓	infant formula
Chicken of the Sea	RAL	✗	(✓)	✗	(✓)	(✓)	No	No	✗	✗	dolphins caught
De Jeans	BN	✗	✓	✓	✓	✓	No	Yes●	(✓)	(✓)	

✓ = Top Rating   (✓) = Middle Rating   ✗ = Bottom Rating   ? = Insufficient Information

For a more detailed explanation see key on page 10

FISH, CANNED

Company or Product	Abbr.	💲	⚥	✈	🐇	🌿	🧪	⚛	🕊	🔆	ALERT
Doxsee	BN	✗	✓	No	✓	✓	✓	No	Yes●	✓	
Gorton's	GIS	✓+	✓	No	✓	✓	✓	No	No	✓	
Harris	BN	✗	✓	No	✓	✓	✓	No	Yes●	✓	
Orleans	BN	✗	✓	No	✓	✓	✓	No	Yes●	✓	
Progresso	WH	✓	✓	No	✓	✗	✓	No	No	?	
StarKist	HNZ	✓	✗	No	✓	✓	✗	No	Yes	✓	dolphins caught
Underwood	WH	✓	✓	No	✓◯	✓	✗	No	No	?	
FLOUR											
Arrowhead Mills#	AM	?	✓	No	✓	✓	✓	No	No	✓	
Aunt Jemima	OAT	✓	✓	No	✓	✓	✓	No	No	✓	
Bakemaster	ADM	?	✓	No	✓	?	✓	No	No	✗	
Buckeye	OAT	✓	✓	No	✓	✓	✓	No	No	✓	

Company or Product	Abbr.	$									ALERT
Eden #	EDEN	✗	✗	No	✓	✓	No	✓	✓	✗	
Fearn Natural Foods #	MOD	?	?	No	✓	◐	No	✓	?	?	
Gold Medal	GIS	✓+	✓	No	✓	✓	No	◐	◐	✓	
King Midas	CAG	?	◐	No	◐	✗	?	◐	◐	?	OSHA fines
Masterstroke	GMP	?	?	?	✗	✗	Yes†	?	?	◐	dolphins caught
Mother's Best	BTC	✓+	◐	No	◐	◐	No	◐	◐	◐	
Ovenjoy	SAFE	?	?	◐	✓	✓	No	✓	◐	◐	
Pillsbury's Best	GMP	?	?	No	◐	✗	Yes†	◐	?	◐	dolphins caught
Quaker	OAT	✓	✓	No	✓	✓	No	?	✓	✓	
Red Brand	GIS	✓+	✓	No	✓	◐	No	✓	✓	◐	

✓ = Top Rating ◐ = Middle Rating ✗ = Bottom Rating ? = Insufficient Information		Page 111
For a more detailed explanation see key on page 10		

FLOUR

Company or Product	Abbr.	$	♀♂	✈	(No)	🐇	✊	⚛	🌍	ALERT
Silver Ribbon	GIS	✓+	✓	✓	No	✓	✓	No	✓	
FROZEN BAKED GOODS										
Aunt Fanny's	WH	✓	✓	✓	No	✓○	✓	No	?	
Aunt Jemima	OAT	✓	✓	✓	No	✓	✓	No	✓	
Barbara's Bakery#	BARB	?	✓	✓	No	✓	✓	No	✗	
Downyflake	WH	✓	✓	✓	No	✓○	✓	No	✓	
Eggo	K	✓	✓	✓	?	?	✗	Yes●	✓	
Great Starts	CPB	✓	✓	✓	No	✓	✓	No	✓	on-site daycare
Hungry Jack	GMP	?	✓	?	?	?	✗	Yes†	?	dolphins caught
Kellogg's	K	✓	✓	✓	No	✓	✓	Yes●	✓	
Lender's Bagels	MO	✗	✗	✓	No	✗	✗	Yes	✗	cigarettes
	GIS	?	?	?	No	?	✓	No	?	OSHA fines

Company or Product	Abbr.	💲	♀						⚛			ALERT
Nature's Own	FLO	?	✗	?	No	?	No	?	No	?	✗	✓	
Nutri-Grain	K	✓	✓	✓	No	✓	✓	No	Yes●	?	✓	✓	
Pepperidge Farm	CPB	✓	✓	✓	No	✓	✓	No	No	?	✓	✓	on-site daycare
Pet-Ritz	WH	✓	✓	✓	No	✓○	✗	No	No	?	✓	✓	
Pie in Minutes	K	✓	✓	✓	No	?	✓	No	Yes●	?	✓	✓	
Pillsbury	GMP	?	?	?	No	?	✗	?	Yes†	?	✓	?	dolphins caught
Sara Lee	SLE	✓	✓	?	No	✓	✓	No	Yes	?	✓	✓	
Stillwell	FLO	?	✗	?	No	?	?	No	No	?	✗	✗	
Swanson	CPB	✓	✓	✓	No	✓	✓	No	No	?	✓	✓	on-site daycare
Toaster Strudel	GMP	?	?	?	No	?	✗	?	Yes†	?	✓	?	dolphins caught

✓ = Top Rating ✓ = Middle Rating ✗ = Bottom Rating ? = Insufficient Information
For a more detailed explanation see key on page 10

FROZEN BAKED GOODS

FROZEN DINNERS

Company or Product	Abbr.	$	♀	👥	🕊	🐾	⚛	👪	🌸	ALERT
FROZEN DINNERS										
A La Carte	MO	✗	✓	✓	No	✓	✓	No	✗	?	cigarettes
Applause	MO	✗	✓	✓	No	✓	✓	No	✗	?	cigarettes
Armour Classics	CAG	?	✓	✓	No	✗	✓	No	✓	?	OSHA fines
Banquet	CAG	?	✓	✓	No	✗	✓	No	✓	?	OSHA fines
Bird's Eye	MO	✗	✓	✓	No	✓	✓	No	✗	?	cigarettes
Bluebox	MO	✗	✓	✓	No	✓	✓	No	✗	?	cigarettes
Cajun Cookin'	WH	✓	✓	✓	No	✓◯	✓	No	?	✓	
Celeste	OAT	✓	✓	✓	No	✓	✓	No	✓	✗	
Chicken Originals	TYSN	?	✓	✗	No	✓	✗	No	✓	✓	
Chun King	CAG	?	✓	✓	No	✗	✓	No	✓	?	OSHA fines
Classic	GMP	?	?	?	No	?	✗	Yes†	?	?	dolphins caught

Company or Product	Abbr.	$	♀	(icon)	(icon)	(icon)	⚛	(icon)	(icon)	(icon)	ALERT
Culinova	MO	✗	✓	✓	?	✓	No	✗	Yes	No	cigarettes
Dinner Supreme	NEST	?	?	?	No	?	No	?	Yes†	✓	infant formula
Fresh Creations	MO	✗	✓	✓	No	✓	No	✗	Yes	No	cigarettes
Frozen Singles	HRL	✓	✓	✗	No	✓	No	✓	No	✗	labor disputes
Gourmet Selection	TYSN	?	✓	✗	No	✓	No	✗	No	✗	
Grande Dinners	BUD	✓+	✓	✓	No	✓	No	✓	No	✓	
Green Giant	GMP	?	?	?	No	✗	No	?	Yes†	?	dolphins caught
Groko	CPB	✓	✓	✓	No	✓	No	✓	No	✓	on-site daycare
Homestyle Recipe	CPB	✓	✓	✓	No	✓	No	✓	No	✓	on-site daycare
Jeno's	GMP	?	?	?	No	✗	No	?	Yes†	?	dolphins caught

✓ = Top Rating   ✓ = Middle Rating   ✗ = Bottom Rating   ? = Insufficient Information

For a more detailed explanation see key on page 10

FROZEN DINNERS

FROZEN DINNERS

Company or Product	Abbr.	💲	♀	👥	✈	🐰	🌿	⚛	👨‍👩‍👧	🕊	ALERT
Kraft Entrees	MO	✗	✓	✓	No	✓	✓	Yes	✗	?	cigarettes
La Choy	BTC	✓+	✓	✓	No	?	?	No	✓	✓	
Le Menu	CPB	✓	✓	✓	No	✓	✓	No	✓	✓	on-site daycare
Le Gout	K	✓	✓	✓	No	✓	✓	Yes●	✓	✓	
Lean Cuisine	NEST	?	✓	✓	No	✓	✗	Yes†	?	✓	infant formula
Lunch Bucket	G	?	✓	✓	No	✓	✓	No	✓	?●	
Old El Paso	WH	✓	✓	✓	No	?	✗	No	?	✓	
Patio	CAG	?	✓	✓	No	✗	✓	No	✓	?	OSHA fines
Pepperidge Farm	CPB	✓	✓	✓	No	✓	✓	No	✓	✓	on-site daycare
Pillsbury	GMP	?	✓	?	No	✗	?	Yes†	?	?	dolphins caught
Ronzoni	MO	✗	✓	✓	No	✓	✓	Yes	✗	?	cigarettes
Savory Classics	OAT	✓	✓	✓	No	✓	✓	No	✓	✓	

Company or Product	Abbr.	$	♀						⚛	♻	ALERT
Stillwell	FLO	?	✗	?	?	✓	?	No	?	✗	
Stouffer's	NEST	?	?	?	✗	✓	?	Yes†	?	✓	infant formula
Swanson Gourmet	CPB	✓	✓	✓	✓	✓	✓	No	✓	✓	on-site daycare
The Gourmet	MO	✗	✓	?	✓	✓	✓	Yes	✗	?	cigarettes
Tombstone	MO	✗	✓	?	✓	✓	✓	Yes	✗	?	cigarettes
Top Shelf	HRL	✓	✗	✓	✗	✓	✗	No	?	✗	labor disputes
Tortino's	GMP	?	?	?	?	✗	?	Yes†	?	?	dolphins caught
Tyson	TYSN	?	✗	✓	✗	✓	✗	No	?	✗	
Velveeta Shells & Cheese	MO	✗	✓	?	✓	✓	✓	Yes	✗	?	cigarettes
Weight Watchers	HNZ	✓	✓	✓	✓	✓	✓	No	✓	✓	dolphins caught

✓ = Top Rating   ✓ = Middle Rating   ✗ = Bottom Rating   ? = Insufficient Information

For a more detailed explanation see key on page 10

FROZEN DINNERS

Company or Product	Abbr.	$	♀	⬚	✈	⬚	⬚	⚛	🌐	ALERT
White Rose	DLG	?	✓	?	No	✓	?	No	✗	

FROZEN JUICES & DRINKS

Company or Product	Abbr.	$	♀	⬚	✈	⬚	⬚	⚛	🌐	ALERT
Bacardi	KO	✓	✓	✓	No	✓	✓	No	✓	
Chiquita	UB	✓	✓	✓	No	✓	✗	No	?	labor disputes
Citrus Hill	PG	✓	✓	✓	No	✓(*)	✓	No	✓	disposable diapers
Dole	CKE	?	✗	?	No	✗	✗	No	?	pesticide use
Five Alive	KO	✓	✓	✓	No	✓	✓	No	✓	
Hawaiian Punch	RJR	✓	✓	?	No	✓	?	Yes*	✗	cigarettes
Minute Maid	KO	✓	✓	✓	No	✓	✓	No	✓	
Snowkist	GIS	✓+	✓	✓	No•	✓	✓	No•	✓	
Squeeze Fresh	KO	✓	✓	✓	No	✓	?	Yes	✓	
Tropicana	VO	?	?	✓	No	✓	?	No	?	

FROZEN MEAT, CHICKEN AND FISH

Company or Product	Abbr.	$	♀	⬛	⚛			No			ALERT
FROZEN MEAT, CHICKEN AND FISH											
Chick 'n Quick	TYSN	?	✓	✗	No	✓	✗	No	✓	✗	
ConAgra	CAG	?	✓	?	No	✗	✓	No	✓	?	OSHA fines
Cornish	TYSN	?	✓	✗	No	✓	✗	No	✓	✗	
Country Pride	CAG	?	✓	?	No	✗	✓	No	✓	?	OSHA fines
Fishamajig	HSY	✓	✓	✓	No	?	✓	No	✓	✓	
Flyers	TYSN	?	✗	✓	No	✓	✗	No	✓	✗	
Gorton's	GIS	✓+	✓	✓	No	?	✓	No	✓	✓	
Holly Farms	HFF	?	✗	✗	No	?	?	No	✗	?	
Louis Kemp	MO	✗	✓	✓	No	✓	✓	Yes	✗	?	cigarettes

✓ = Top Rating ✓ = Middle Rating ✗ = Bottom Rating ? = Insufficient Information

For a more detailed explanation see key on page 10

FROZEN MEAT, CHICKEN AND FISH

FROZEN MEAT, CHICKEN AND FISH

Company or Product	Abbr.	💲	♀	👥	🐦	🏃	🐾	⚛	✡	ALERT
Morton	CAG	?	✓	✓	No	✗	✓	No	?	?	OSHA fines
Mrs. Paul's	CPB	✓	✓	✓	No	✓	✓	No	✓	✓	on-site daycare
Steak-Umm	HNZ	✓	✓	✗	Yes	✓	✓	No	✗	✓	dolphins caught
Taste o' Sea	CAG	?	✓	✓	No	✗	✓	No	?	?	OSHA fines
Van de Kamp's	GMP	?	?	?	No	✗	?	Yes†	?	?	dolphins caught
Weaver	HFF	?	✗	✗	No	✗	?	No	✗	?	

FROZEN VEGETABLES & POTATOES

Company or Product	Abbr.	💲	♀	👥	🐦	🏃	🐾	⚛	✡	ALERT
Americana Recipe	MO	✗	✓	✓	No	✓	✓	No	✗	?	cigarettes
Bird's Eye	MO	✗	✓	✓	No	✓	✓	No	✗	?	cigarettes
Blue Ribbon	MO	✗	✓	✓	No	✓	✓	No	✗	?	cigarettes
Country Stand	RAL	✓	✗	✓	No	✓	✓	No	✓	✗	dolphins caught
Crispers	HNZ	✓	✗	✓	Yes	✓	✓	Yes	✓	✓	dolphins caught

FROZEN VEGETABLES & POTATOES

Company or Product	Abbr.	💲	♀						⚛					ALERT
Crosscuts	UFC	✓	✓	✗	?	No	✓	✓	?	?	No	?	?	
Curly Q	UFC	✓	✓	✗	?	No	✓	✓	?	?	No	?	?	
Dawn Fresh	GMP	?	?	?	?	?	✗	?	?	?	Yes†	?	?	dolphins caught
Farm Fresh	MO	✗	✓	✓	?	No	✓	✓	No	✗	Yes	?	?	cigarettes
Festival	WF	?	?	?	?	No	✓	?	No	?	No	?	✗	
Garden Gourmet	GMP	?	?	?	?	?	✗	?	?	?	Yes†	?	?	dolphins caught
Green Giant	GMP	?	?	?	?	?	✗	?	?	?	Yes†	?	?	dolphins caught
Hain Naturals	WH	✓	✓	?	No	✓⃝	✓	✓	✗	?	No	✓	✓	
Health Valley Nat. Foods#	HVAL	?	✓	?	No	?	?	?	?	No	No	✓	✗	
Heinz	HNZ	✓	✓	✗	No	✓	✓	✓	No	✓	Yes	✓	✓	dolphins caught

✓ = Top Rating ⌇ = Middle Rating ✗ = Bottom Rating ? = Insufficient Information

For a more detailed explanation see key on page 10

FROZEN VEGETABLES & POTATOES

Company or Product	Abbr.	💲	⚥				⚛				ALERT
Inland Valley	UFC	✓	✓	✗	No	✓	?	?	No	?	?	
Kountry Kist	GMP	?	?	?	?	?	✓	?	Yes†	?	?	dolphins caught
Long-Branch Fries	UFC	✓	✓	✗	No	✓	?	?	No	?	?	
Luck's	AHP	✗	✓†	✗	No	✓(*)	✓	✓	Yes*	✗	✗	infant formula
McKenzie's	CBI	✓+	✓	?	No	?	✓	?	No	?	✓	
Ore Ida	HNZ	✓	✓	✗	No	✓	✓	✓	Yes	✓	✓	dolphins caught
Oven Q	UFC	✓	✓	✗	No	✓	?	?	No	?	?	
Special Additions	GMP	?	?	?	?	✗	✓	?	Yes†	?	?	dolphins caught
Spud Skin	UFC	✓	✓	✗	No	✓	✓	?	No	?	?	
Spudsville	NEST	?	?	?	?	?	?	?	Yes†	✗	✓	infant formula
Stillwell	FLO	?	✗	?	No	?	✓	?	No	?	✗	
Tiny Taters	MO	✗	✓	✗	No	✓	?	✗	Yes	?	?	cigarettes

Company or Product	Abbr.	💲	⚥	⚛	✈	🏭	⚗	☢	🐇	ALERT
Toaster Browns	OAT	✔	✔	✔	No	✔	✔	No	✔	
Vegetable Classics	RJR	✔	✔	✓	No	✓	?	Yes*	✗	cigarettes
White Rose	DIG	?	✓	✓	No	✓	?	No	✗	
FRUIT, CANNED										
Dole	CKE	?	✗	?	No	✗	?	No	?	pesticide use
Deana	HFF	?	✗	?	No	✗	?	No	?	
Del Monte	RJR	✔	✓	✓	No	✓	?	Yes*	✗	cigarettes
Eden#	EDEN	✗	✗	✓	No	✗	✓	No	✗	
Cherry Hill#	CHER	?	✓	✓	No	✓	✓	No	?	
Geobe	HFF	?	✗	?	No	✗	?	No	?	

✔ = Top Rating   ✓ = Middle Rating   ✗ = Bottom Rating   ? = Insufficient Information

For a more detailed explanation see key on page 10

FRUIT, CANNED

Company or Product	Abbr.	💲	♀	✈	🐇	✊	👥	⚛	🌍	🕊	ALERT
Libby's	NEST	?	?	No	No	?	?	No	No	Yes†	✓	infant formula
Mott's	CADB	✓	?	✗	?	No	✓	?	No	Yes†	✓	
Ocean Spray	OSC	?	?	?	?	No	?	?	No	No	?	
Thank You Brand	CBI	✓+	?	✓	No	?	?	?	No	No	✓	

HAIR CARE NEEDS

Company or Product	Abbr.	💲	♀	✈	🐇	✊	👥	⚛	🌍	🕊	ALERT
Adorn	GS	✓	✓	No	✓	?	✓	?	No	Yes●	✓	
Affinity	JNJ	✓	✓	No	✓(*)	✓	✓	?	No	Yes*	✓	
Afro-Sheen	JPC	?	?	No	✗	?	?	No	No	No	✗	
Agree	SCJ	✓+	✓	No	✗	✓	✓	?	No	Yes●	✓	1st to ban CFC's
Alberto VO5	ACV	?	?	No	✗	?	?	?	No	No	?	
Aqua Body	FAB	?	?	No	✗	?	?	?	No	No	?	
Aubrey Organics#	AUB	?	✓	No	✓	?	?	?	No	No	✓	

Company or Product	Abbr.	💲	♀	〰️	✈️	🐇	⚛	⚛	🐿️	Yes	🐾	🕊️	ALERT
Biotene H24	CARM	?	✓	✓	No	✓	?	No	✓	Yes	✓	✓	
Body On Tap	BMY	✓	✓	✓	No	✓(*)	✓	No	✓	Yes*	✓	✗	infant formula
Bonsandt	CARM	?	✓	?	No	✓	?	No	✓	Yes	✓	✓	
Breck	ACY	✓	✓	✓	No	✗○	?	No	✓	Yes*	✗	✓	makes pesticides
Carme	CARM	?	✓	✓	No	✓	?	No	✓	Yes	✓	✓	
Clairol	BMY	✓	✓	✓	No	✓(*)	?	No	✓	Yes*	?	✗	infant formula
Classy Curl	JPC	?	?	✓	No	✗	?	No	✓	No	✓	✗	
Clean & Clear	REVL	?	✓	?	No	✓	?	No	✓	Yes●	✓	✓	
Clear Difference	GS	✓	✓	✓	No	✗	✓	No	✓	Yes●	✓	✓	
Country Roads	CARM	?	✓	✓	No	✓	?	No	✓	Yes	✓	✓	

✓ = Top Rating ✓ = Middle Rating ✗ = Bottom Rating ? = Insufficient Information

For a more detailed explanation see key on page 10

HAIR CARE NEEDS

HAIR CARE NEEDS

Company or Product	Abbr.	$	♀	[icon]	✈	[icon]	[icon]	[icon]	⚛	[icon]	[icon]	ALERT
Denorex	AHP	✗	✗	✗	No	✔(*)	✔	✓	No	Yes*	✓	✗	infant formula
Dimension	UN	✗	✗	✓	No	✔*	✔	✗	No	Yes†	?	✓	
Dippity-Do	GS	✓	✓	✔	No	✗	✔	✓	No	Yes●	✔	✓	
Elastin	CARM	?	?	✓	No	✔	✗	?	No	Yes	✓	✓	
Faberge	FAB	?	?	✔	No	✗	✗	?	No	No	✓	?	
Final Net	BMY	✔	✔	✔	No	✔(*)	✔	✓	No	Yes*	?	✗	infant formula
Flex	REVL	✔	?	?	No	✔	✓	?	No	Yes●	✓	✓	
Fresh Hold	BMY	✔	✔	✔	No	✔(*)	✔	✓	No	Yes*	?	✗	infant formula
Gelee	ACV	?	?	✓	No	✗	✗	?	No	No	?	?	
Gentle-Treatment	JPC	?	?	✔	No	✗	✗	?	No	No	✓	✗	
Halsa	SCJ	✔+	✔	✓	No	✗	✔	✔	No	Yes●	✔	✓	1st to ban CFC's
Head & Shoulders	PG	✔	✔	✔	No	✔(*)	✔	✔	No	Yes	✓	✓	disposable diapers

Company or Product	Abbr.	#	♀	✈	✍	🌐	⚛	☢	✿	🐇	ALERT
Herbal Essence	BMY	✓	✓	No	✓*	✓	No	Yes*	?	✗	infant formula
Instant Beauty	BMY	✓	✓	No	✓*	✓	No	Yes*	?	✗	infant formula
Ivory	PG	✓	✓	No	✓*	✓	No	Yes	◐	✓	disposable diapers
Johnson's	JNJ	✓	✓	No	✓*	✓	No	Yes*	✓	✓	
Jojoba Farms	CARM	?	✓	No	✓*	✓	?	Yes	◐	✓	
L'Envie	SCJ	✓+	◐	No	✗	✓	No	Yes●	✓	✓	1st to ban CFC's
La Maur	DOW	◐	◐	No	✓*	◐	Yes	Yes	◐	✓	makes pesticides
Lilt	PG	✓	◐	No	✓*	✓	No	Yes	◐	✓	disposable diapers
Milk Creek	CARM	?	◐	No	✗	?	No	Yes	?	◐	
Mink	GS	✓	✓	No	✗	◐	No	Yes●	✓	✓	

✓ = Top Rating ◐ = Middle Rating ✗ = Bottom Rating ? = Insufficient Information

For a more detailed explanation see key on page 10

HAIR CARE NEEDS

Company or Product	Abbr.	$	♀♂		✈	🐰		⚛			ALERT
Mountain Ocean#	MOUN	?	✓	✗	No	✓	✓	No	✓	✗	
Mountain Herbery	CARM	?	✓	✓	No	✓	✓	Yes	?	✓	
Nice 'n Easy	BMY	✓	✓	✓	No	✓(*)	✓	Yes*	?	✗	infant formula
Orjene Nat. Cosmetics#	ORJ	?	?	?	No	✓*	✗	No	✓	✗	
Palmolive	CL	✓	✓	✓	No	✓*	✓	No	✓	✓	
Pantene	PG	✓+	✓	✓	No	✓(*)	✓	Yes*	✓	✓	
Paul Penders#	PP	?	?	✗	No	✓	✓	No	✓	✓	disposable diapers
Pert	PG	✓	✓	✓	No	✓(*)	✓	Yes	✓	✓	disposable diapers
Prell	PG	✓	✓	✓	No	✓(*)	✓	Yes	✓	✓	disposable diapers
Prescription	BMY	✓	✓	✓	No	✓(*)	✓	Yes*	?	✗	infant formula
Progaine	UPJ	✓	✓	✗	No	○	✗	Yes●	✓	✓	
Rave	UN	✗	✓	✓	No	✓*	✗	Yes†	✓	?	

Company or Product	Abbr.	$	⚥	⚒	🐇	🕊	⚛	✈	☢	ALERT
Replenish	FAB	?	?	?	No	✗	?	No	?	
Reviva Labs#	REV	?	?	?	No	✓	✗	No	✗	
Revlon	REVL	?	?	✓	No	✓	?	Yes●	✓	
Rosa Mosqueta#	AUB	?	✓	✓	No	✓	✓	No	✓	
Selsun Blue	ABT	✗	✓	?	No	✗○	✓	Yes●	✓	infant formula
Shulton	ACY	✓	✓	?	No	✗○	✗	Yes*	✓	makes pesticides
Silkience	GS	✓	✓	✓	No	✗	✓	Yes●	✓	
Sleepy Hollow Botanical	CARM	?	✓	✓	No	✓	?	Yes	✓	
Style Hairspray	DOW	✓	✓	✓	No	✓(*)	✓	Yes	✓	makes pesticides
Thrive	ACY	✓	?	?	No	✗○	✗	Yes*	✗	makes pesticides

✔ = Top Rating   ✓ = Middle Rating   ✗ = Bottom Rating   ? = Insufficient Information

For a more detailed explanation see key on page 10

HAIR CARE NEEDS

Company or Product	Abbr.	💲	⚥	✈	✊	🌍	⚛	🐾	☮	ALERT
Tom's of Maine #	TOM	✓+	✓	✗	No	✓	No	✓	✓	
Toni Lightwaves	GS	✓	✓	✓	No	✓	Yes●	✓	✓	
Twin Labs	TWIN	?	✓	✓	No	?	No	✓	✗	
Ultra Sheen	JPC	?	✓	✗	No	?	No	✓	✗	
Ultra Star	JPC	?	✓	✗	No	?	No	✓	✗	
Ultress	BMY	✓	✓	✓(*)	No	✓	Yes*	?	✗	infant formula
Vitalis	BMY	✓	✓	✓(*)	No	✓	Yes*	?	✗	infant formula
White Rain	GS	✓	✓	✗	No	✓	Yes●	✓	✓	

HOUSEHOLD CLEANING COMPOUNDS & SPONGES

Company or Product	Abbr.	💲	⚥	✈	✊	🌍	⚛	🐾	☮	ALERT
Ajax	CL	✓+	✓	✓*	No	✓	No	✓	✓	
Boyle Midway	AHP	✗	✓	✓(*)	No	✓	Yes*	✓	✗	infant formula
Brillo	G	?	✓	✓	No	✓	No	✓	?	

HOUSEHOLD CLEANING

Company or Product	Abbr.	$	♀		✈			⚛			ALERT
Cameo	G	?	✓	✓	No	✓	✓	No	No	?	
Challenge	CL	✓+	✓	✓	No	✓*	✓	No	Yes*	✓	
Comet	PG	✓	✓	✓	No	✓(*)	✓	No	Yes	✓	disposable diapers
Dow Bathroom Cleaner	DOW	✓	✓	✓	No	✓(*)	✓	Yes	Yes	✓	makes pesticides
Drackett	BMY	✓	✓	✓	No	✓(*)	✓	No	Yes*	✗	infant formula
Drano	BMY	✓	✓	✓	No	✓(*)	✓	No	Yes*	✗	infant formula
Easy Reach	BMY	✓	✓	✓	No	✓(*)	✓	No	Yes*	✗	infant formula
Easy Off	AHP	✗	✓	✗	No	✓(*)	✓	No	Yes*	✗	infant formula
Endust	BMY	✓	✓	✓	No	✓(*)	✓	No	Yes*	✗	infant formula
Fantastik	DOW	✓	✓	✓	No	✓(*)	✓	Yes	Yes	✓	makes pesticides

✓ = Top Rating	✓ = Middle Rating	✗ = Bottom Rating	? = Insufficient Information	**Page 131**

For a more detailed explanation see key on page 10

Company or Product	Abbr.	💲	♀		✈			⚛			ALERT
Formula 409	CLX	✓	✓	✓	No	✓*	✓	No	No	✓	
Glass Plus	DOW	✓	✓	✓	No	✓*	✓	Yes	Yes	✓	makes pesticides
Javex	BMY	✓	✓	✓	No	✓*	✓	No	Yes*	✗	infant formula
Lehn & Fink	EK	✓	✓	✗	Yes	✓*	✓	No	No	✓	
Lestoil	NOXL	✓+	✓	✓	No	✓*	✗	No	No	✓	
Liquid-plumr	CLX	✓	✓	✓	No	✓*	✓	No	No	✓	
Lysoform	UN	✗	✓	✓	No	✓*	✗	No	Yes†	?	
Lysol	EK	✓	✓	✓	Yes	✓*	✓	No	No	✓	
Mr. Muscle	BMY	✓	✓	✓	No	✓*	✓	No	Yes*	?	infant formula
Mr. Clean	PG	✓	✓	✓	No	✓*	✓	No	Yes	✓	disposable diapers
Mrs. Paul's	CPB	✓	✓	✓	No	?	✓	No	No	✓	on-site daycare
Nutrament	BMY	✓	✓	✓	No	✓*	✓	No	Yes*	✗	infant formula

Company or Product	Abbr.	💲	⚥	▨		🏃		⚛		☢	ALERT
O-Cedar	BMY	✓	✓	✓	No	✓*	✓	No	Yes*	?	✗	infant formula
Pine-Sol	ACY	✓	✓	?	No	✗*	✓	?	Yes*	✗	✓	makes pesticides
Red Devil	AHP	✗	✓	✗	No	○*	✓	?	Yes*	✗	✗	infant formula
Renuzit	BMY	✓	✓	✓	No	✓*	✓	?	Yes*	?	✗	infant formula
S.O.S.	MILS	?	?	?	No	✗○	?	?	Yes†	?	✗	infant formula
Sail	GAP	?	✓	✓	No	✓	?	✓	No	✓	✓	refuses cans
Sani-Flush	AHP	✗	✓	✗	No	✓*	✓	✓	Yes*	✓	✗	infant formula
Scotch-Brite	SPP	✓	✓	✓	No	✗*	✓	✓	No	✗	✓	forestry criticized
Scrunge	CRCH	?	✓	?	No	✓*	✓	✓	No	✓	✓	
Sno Bowl	G	?	✓	✓	No	✓	✓	✓	No	?	?	

✓ = Top Rating   ✗ = Bottom Rating   ✓ = Middle Rating   ? = Insufficient Information

For a more detailed explanation see key on page 10

HOUSEHOLD CLEANING

Page 133

Company or Product	Abbr.	$	♀					⚛		✡	ALERT
Soft Scrub	CLX	✓	✓	✓	No	✓*	✓	No	No	✓	
Soft Scour	MMM	✓	✓	✓	No	✓*	✓	No	Yes*	✓	
Spic & Span	PG	✓	✓	✓	No	✓*	✓	No	Yes	✓	disposable diapers
Stretch 'n Dust	JNJ	✓	✓	✓	No	✓*	✓	No	Yes*	✓	
Tackle	CLX	✓	✓	✓	No	✓*	✓	No	No	✓	
Texize	DOW	✓	✓	✓	No	✓*	✓	Yes	Yes	✓	makes pesticides
Tilex	CLX	✓	✓	✓	No	✓*	✓	No	No	✓	
Top Job	PG	✓	✓	✓	No	✓*	✓	No	Yes	✓	disposable diapers
Tough Act	DOW	✓	✓	✓	No	✓*	✓	Yes	Yes	✓	makes pesticides
Vanish	BMY	✓	✓	✓	No	✓*	✓	No	Yes*	?	✗	infant formula
Windex	BMY	✓	✓	✓	No	✓*	✓	No	Yes*	?	✗	infant formula

HOUSEHOLD SUPPLIES

Company or Product	Abbr.											ALERT
6/12 Plus	EK	✔	✔	✔	✔	Yes	✔⊛	✔	No	✔	✔	
Acme	ASC	?	✔	✔	✓	No	✔	✓	No	?	?	
Arm & Hammer	CRCH	?	✔	✓	?	No	✓*	✓	No	✔	✓	
Black Flag	AHP	✗	✗	✔	✗	No	✔⊛	✓	Yes*	✗	✗	infant formula
Boyle Midway	AHP	✗	✗	✔	✗	No	✔⊛	✓	Yes*	✓	✗	infant formula
Brite	SCJ	✔+	✔	✔	✔	No	✗	✔	Yes●	✔	✔	1st to ban CFC's
Combat	ACY	✔	✔	✔	?	No	✗○	?	Yes*	✗	✓	makes pesticides
d-Con	EK	✔	✔	✔	✔	Yes	✔⊛	✔	No	✔	✔	
Dial	G	?	✔	✓	✓	No	✔	✓	No	✔	?	

✔ = Top Rating   ✓ = Middle Rating   ✗ = Bottom Rating   ? = Insufficient Information
For a more detailed explanation see key on page 10

HOUSEHOLD SUPPLIES

Company or Product	Abbr.	💲	♀	✈	🧴	⚛	🐢	ALERT
Drackett	BMY	✓	✓	No	✓(*)	No	Yes*	?	✗	infant formula
Dry Breezes	AHP	✗	✓	✗	✓(*)	No	Yes*	✓	✗	infant formula
Duster Plus	SCJ	✓+	✓	✓	✗	No	Yes●	✓	✓	1st to ban CFC's
Elmer's	BN	✗	✓	✓	✓	No	Yes●	✓	✓	
Energizer	RAL	✗	✓	✗	✓	No	No	✓	✗	dolphins caught
Eveready	RAL	✗	✓	✗	✓	No	No	✓	✗	dolphins caught
Flair	GS	✓	✓	No	✓	No	Yes●	✓	✓	
Flie	GS	✓	✓	No	✗	No	Yes●	✓	✓	
Future	SCJ	✓+	✓	No	✗	No	Yes●	✓	✓	1st to ban CFC's
GE	GE	✓	✓	Yes*	✓	Yes	Yes	✓	✗	INFACT Boycott
Glade	SCJ	✓+	✓	No	✗	No	Yes●	✓	✓	1st to ban CFC's
GloCoat	SCJ	✓+	✓	No	✗	No	Yes●	✓	✓	1st to ban CFC's

Company or Product	Abbr.	💲	⚥	🧑	✈	⚗	⚛	🐇	⚛	👶🐱	⚙	ALERT
GTE	GTE	✗	◡	?	Yes*	◡	◡	◡	No	Yes	◡	◡	
Johnson & Johnson	JNJ	◡	◡	◡	No	✓(*)	◡	✓	No	Yes*	✓	✓	
Johnson Wax	SCJ	✓+	◡	◡	No	✗	✓	✓	No	Yes*●	✓	✓	1st to ban CFC's
K2r	DOW	✓	◡	✓	No	✓(*)	◡	◡	Yes	Yes	◡	✓	makes pesticides
Kingsford	CLX	✓	◡	◡	No	✗	✓	✓	No	No	◡	✓	
Klean 'n Shine	SCJ	✓+	◡	◡	No	✗	✓	✓	No	Yes●	✓	✓	1st to ban CFC's
Krylon	BN	✗	✓	✓	No	✓	✓	◡	No	Yes●	◡	✓	
Lehn & Fink	EK	◡	✓	✓	Yes	✓(*)	✓	✓	No	No	✓	✓	
Lysol	EK	◡	✓	✓	Yes	✓(*)	✓	✓	No	No	✓	✓	
Miniwax	EK	◡	✓	✓	Yes	✓(*)	✓	✓	No	No	◡	✓	

✓ = Top Rating   ◡ = Middle Rating   ✗ = Bottom Rating   ? = Insufficient Information

For a more detailed explanation see key on page 10

HOUSEHOLD SUPPLIES

HOUSEHOLD SUPPLIES

Company or Product	Abbr.	💲	♀	🏳	✈	🐰	✋	🐎	⚛	👥	🌐	ALERT
Miser	GE	✓	✓	✓	Yes*	✗	✓	✓	Yes	✗	✓	INFACT Boycott
Mop & Glow	EK	✓	✓	✓	Yes	✓(*)	✓	✓	No	✓	✓	
Noxon	AHP	✗	✓	✗	No	✓(*)	✓	✓	Yes*	✓	✗	infant formula
Off!	SCJ	✓+	✓	✓	No	✓(*)	✓	✓	No	✓	✓	1st to ban CFC's
Old English	AHP	✗	✓	✗	No	✓(*)	✓	✓	Yes*	✓	✗	infant formula
Parson's	G	?	✓	✓	No	✓	✓	✓	No	✓	?	
Pencil Mate	GS	✓	✓	✓	No	✗	✓	✓	Yes●	✓	✓	
Perk	RAL	✗	✓	✗	No	✓	✓	✓	No	✗	✗	dolphins caught
Pledge	SCJ	✓+	✓	✓	No	✓	✓	✓	Yes●	✗	✓	1st to ban CFC's
Polaroid	PRD	✓+	✓	✓	No	✗	✓	✓	No	✓	✓	
Pronto	SCJ	✓+	✓	✓	No	✗	✓	✓	Yes●	✗	✓	1st to ban CFC's
Raid	SCJ	✓+	✓	✓	No	✗	✓	✓	Yes●	✗	✓	1st to ban CFC's

Company or Product	Abbr.	$	⚥							⚛				ALERT
Resinite	BN	✗	✓	✓	✓	No	✓	✓	✓	No	Yes●	?	?	
Resolve	EK	✓	✓	✓	?	Yes	✓(*)	✓	✓	No	No	?	✓	
RIT	CPC	✗	✓	✓	?	No	✓	✓	?	No	No	?	?	
Scotch	MMM	?	✓	✓	✓	No	✓*	✓	✓	No	Yes●	✓	✓	
Seal Wrap	BN	✗	✓	✓	?	No	✓	✓	✓	No	Yes●	?	?	
Shell	SC	✓	✓	✓	?	Yes	✓*	✗	✓	No	Yes†	✓	✓	
Shout	SCJ	✓+	✓	?	?	No	✗	✓	✓	No	Yes●	✓	✓	1st to ban CFC's
Spectra	PRD	✓+	✓	✓	?	No	✓	✓	✓	No	No	?	✓	
Step Saver	SCJ	✓+	✓	✓	?	No	✗	✓	✓	No	Yes●	✓	✓	1st to ban CFC's
Sterling Drug	EK	✓	✓	✓	?	No	✓(*)	✓	✓	No	No	?	✓	

✓ = Top Rating ✓ = Middle Rating ✗ = Bottom Rating ? = Insufficient Information
For a more detailed explanation see key on page 10

HOUSEHOLD SUPPLIES

JAMS, JELLIES, AND SPREADS

Company or Product	Abbr.	💲	⚥	🪖	✈	🌍	✊	⚛	🐰	🌿	ALERT
Sylvania	GTE	✗	✓	?	Yes*	✓	✓	No	✓	✓	
Tegon	MO	✗	✓	✓	No	✓	✓	No	✗	?	cigarettes
Woolite	AHP	✗	✗	✗	No	✓(*)	✓	No	✓*	✗	infant formula

JAMS, JELLIES, AND SPREADS

Company or Product	Abbr.	💲	⚥	🪖	✈	🌍	✊	⚛	🐰	🌿	ALERT
Arrowhead Mills#	AM	?	✓	?	No	✓	?	No	✓	✓	
Bama	BN	✗	✓	✗	No	✓	✓	No	Yes●	✓	
Cherry Hill#	CHER	?	✓	✗	No	✓	✓	No	✓	?	
Crosse & Blackwell	NEST	?	?	?	No	✓	✗	No	Yes†	✓	infant formula
Eden#	EDEN	✗	✓	✗	No	✓	✓	No	✓	✗	
Frank Cooper	CPC	✗	✗	✓	No	✓	✓	No	✓	✓	
Health Valley Nat. Foods#	HVAL	?	✓	✓	No	✓	?	No	✓	✗	
Jif	PG	✓	✓	✓	No	✓(*)	✓	Yes	✓	✓	disposable diapers

Company or Product	Abbr.									ALERT
Laura Scudder's	BN	✗	✓	No	✓	✓	No	Yes●	✓	
Lifetone International#	LFTI	?	✗	No	✗	✗	No	✓	?	
Panhandler Conserves#	CHER	?	✓	No	✓	✓	No	✓	?	
Peter Pan	BTC	✓+	?	No	?	?	No	✓	✓	
Simply Fruit	SJM	✓	✓	No	✓	✓	No	✓	✗	
Skippy	CPC	✗	✓	No	✓	✓	No	✓	✓	
Smucker's	SJM	✓	✓	No	✓	✓	No	✓	✓	
Super Krunch	MO	✗	✓	No	✓	✗	No	Yes	✗	cigarettes

JUICE AND JUICE DRINKS

Company or Product	Abbr.									ALERT
Apple & Eve#	APNE	?	✗	✗	No	✓	?	No	No	?	✗

✓ = Top Rating   ✓ = Middle Rating   ✗ = Bottom Rating   ? = Insufficient Information

For a more detailed explanation see key on page 10

Page 141

JUICE AND JUICE DRINKS

JUICE AND JUICE DRINKS

Company or Product	Abbr.	$	♀	⚒	🔫	🐢	🌍	⚛	👪	🕊	ALERT
Bright & Early	KO	✓	✓	✓	No	?	✓	No	Yes	✓	
Campbell's	CPB	✓	✓	✓	No	?	✓	No	No	✓	on-site daycare
Chiquita	UB	?	?	?	No	?	?	No	No	✗	
Citrus Hill Select	PG	✓	✓	✓	No	✓(*)	✓	No	Yes	✓	disposable diapers
Clamato	CADB	✓	✓	✗	No	?	✓	No	Yes†	?	
Country Time	MO	✓	✓	✓	No	?	✓	No	Yes	?	cigarettes
Crystal Light	MO	✓	✓	✓	No	?	✓	No	Yes	?	cigarettes
Del Monte	RJR	✓	✗	✓	No	?	?	No	Yes*	✗	cigarettes
Dole	CKE	?	?	?	No	?	✗	No	No	?	pesticide use
Five Alive	KO	✓	✓	✓	No	?	✓	No	Yes	✓	
Fruit Juicer	GIS	✓+	✓	✓	No	?	✓	No	No	✓	
Gatorade	OAT	✓	✓	✓	No	✓	✓	No	No	✓	

Company or Product	Abbr.											ALERT
Hawaiian Punch	RJR	✔	✔	?	No	?	✔	?	No	Yes*	✘	cigarettes
Hi-C	KO	✔	✔	✔	No	?	✔	✔	No	Yes	✔	
Joe's#	DVF	✘	✘	?	No	✔	✔	?	No	No	✘	infant formula
Juicy Juice	NEST	?	?	?	No	✔	✘	✔	No	Yes†	?	infant formula
Libby's	NEST	?	?	?	No	✔	✘	✔	No	Yes†	✔	
Lipton	UN	✔	✔	✔	No	✔*	✘	✔	No	Yes†	✔	
Minute Maid	KO	✔	✔	✔	No	?	✔	✔	No	Yes	?	
Mott's	CADB	✔	✔	✔	No	?	✔	✔	No	Yes†	✔	
Natura#	NFS	?	?	?	No	?	✔	✔	No	No	?	
Nestea	NEST	?	?	?	No	?	✘	✔	No	Yes†	✔	infant formula

✔ = Top Rating ✓ = Middle Rating ✘ = Bottom Rating ? = Insufficient Information

For a more detailed explanation see key on page 10

Page 143

JUICE AND JUICE DRINKS

JUICE AND JUICE DRINKS

Company or Product	Abbr.	💲	⚥	👥	🖐	✈	🧍	✊	⚛	🐢	ALERT
Ocean Spray	OSC	?	?	?	✔	No	?	✘	No	?	
ReaLemon	BN	✘	✔	✔	✔	No	✔	✔	Yes●	✔	
ReaLime	BN	✘	✔	✔	✔	No	✔	✔	Yes●	✔	
Red Cheek	CADB	✔	✔	✘	✔	No	✔	✔	Yes†	?†	
Sunkist	RJR	✔	✔	✔	✔	No	?	✔	Yes✱	✘	cigarettes
Tang	MO	✘	✔	✔	✔	No	✔	✔	Yes	✘	cigarettes
Tropicana	VO	?	?	✔	?	No	?	✔	No	✔	
V8	CPB	✔	✔	✔	✔	No	✔	✔	No	✔	on-site daycare
White Rose	DIG	?	?	✔	✔	No	?	?	No	✔	
Wyler's	MO	✘	✔	✔	✔	No	✔	✘	Yes	?	cigarettes

LAUNDRY SUPPLIES

LAUNDRY SUPPLIES

Company or Product	Abbr.	💲	♀	✊	✈	🤖	💪	⚛	🌐	♻	ALERT
All	UN	✗	✓	✓	No	✓*	✗	No	Yes†	?	
Arm & Hammer	CRCH	?	✓	✓	No	✓*	✓	No	No	✓	
Bold	PG	✓	✓	✓	No	✓(*)	✓	Yes	Yes	✓	disposable diapers
Borateem	G	?	✓	✓	No	✓	✓	No	No	?	
Bounce	PG	✓	✓	✓	No	✓(*)	✓	Yes	Yes	✓	disposable diapers
Boyle Midway	AHP	✗	✗	✓	No	✓(*)	✓	No	Yes*	✗	infant formula
Cheer	PG	✓	✓	✓	No	✓(*)	✓	Yes	Yes	✓	disposable diapers
Cling Free	BECH	?	?	?	No	✗(*)	?	No	Yes†	?	
Clorox	CLX	✓	✓	✓	No	✓*	✓	No	No	✓	
Dash	PG	✓	✓	✓	No	✓(*)	✓	Yes	Yes	✓	disposable diapers

✓ = Top Rating ✓ = Middle Rating ✗ = Bottom Rating ? = Insufficient Information

For a more detailed explanation see key on page 10

LAUNDRY SUPPLIES

Company or Product	Abbr.	$	⚧	🐇	✈	🧪	♻	⚛	⚠	🌸	ALERT
Delicare	BECH	?	?	?	No	✗○	?	No	Yes†	?	
Downy	PG	✓	✓	✓	No	✓(*)	✓	No	Yes	✓	disposable diapers
Dreft	PG	✓	✓	✓	No	✓(*)	✓	No	Yes	✓	disposable diapers
Dynamo 2	CL	✓+	✓	✓	No	✓*	✓	No	Yes*	✓	
Easy Off	AHP	✗	✗	✓	No	✓(*)	✓	No	Yes*	✗	infant formula
Era	PG	✓	✓	✓	No	✓(*)	✓	No	Yes	✓	disposable diapers
Fab	CL	✓+	✓	✓	No	✓*	✓	No	Yes*	✓	
Final Touch	UN	✗	✓	✓	No	✓*	✗	No	Yes†	?	
Fresh Start	CL	✓+	✓	✓	No	✓*	✓	No	Yes*	✓	
Grease Relief	DOW	✓	✓	✓	No	✓(*)	✓	Yes	Yes	✓	makes pesticides
Ivory Snow	PG	✓	✓	✓	No	✓(*)	✓	No	Yes	✓	disposable diapers

Company or Product	Abbr.	$	♀	✊	✈	✋	🐾	⚛	⚛/Yes	⚖	🌐	ALERT
Johnson Wax	SCJ	✔+	✓	✓	No	✓	✘	✔	No	Yes●	✔	✔	1st to ban CFC's
Joy	PG	✓	✓	✓	No	✔⊛	✓	✓	No	Yes	✓	✔	disposable diapers
Niagara	CPC	✘	✓	✓	No	✓	✓	✓	No	No	✓		
Purex	G	?	✓	✓	No	✓	✓	✓	No	No	?		
Shout	SCJ	✔+	✓	✓	No	✔*	✘	✔	No	Yes●	✔	✔	1st to ban CFC's
Snuggle	UN	✘	✓	✓	No	✔⊛	✓	✓	No	Yes†	?	?	
Solo	PG	✓	✓	✓	No	✔⊛	✓	✓	No	Yes	✔	✔	disposable diapers
Spray 'n Starch	DOW	✓	✓	✓	No	✓	✓	✓	Yes	Yes	✓	✔	makes pesticides
Spray 'n Wash	DOW	✓	✓	✓	No	✔⊛	✓	✓	Yes	Yes	✓	✔	makes pesticides
Static-Guard	ACV	?	?	?	No	✘	?	✘	No	No	?	?	

✔ = Top Rating   ✓ = Middle Rating   ✘ = Bottom Rating   ? = Insufficient Information

For a more detailed explanation see key on page 10

LAUNDRY SUPPLIES

LAUNDRY SUPPLIES

Company or Product	Abbr.	💲	♀	✊	✈	⛷	☮	⚛	🕊	🌐	🐇	ALERT
Surf	UN	✗	✓	✓	No	✓*	✓	No	Yes†	?	✓	?	
Tide	PG	✓	✓	✓	No	✓(*)	✓	No	Yes	✓	✓	✓	disposable diapers
Vivid	DOW	✓	✓	✓	No	✓(*)	✓	Yes	Yes	✓	✓	✓	makes pesticides
Wash a bye Baby	CL	✓+	✓	✓	No	✓*	✓	No	Yes*	✓	✓	✓	
Wash 'N Dry	CL	✓+	✓	✓	No	✓*	✓	No	Yes*	✓	✓	✓	
Wisk	UN	✗	✓	✓	No	✓*	✗	No	Yes†	?	✓	?	
Woolite	AHP	✗	✗	✗	No	✓(*)	✓	No	Yes*	✓	✓	✗	infant formula
Yes	DOW	✓	✓	✓	No	✓(*)	✓	Yes	Yes	✓	✓	✓	makes pesticides

MARGARINE & BUTTER

Company or Product	Abbr.	💲	♀	✊	✈	⛷	☮	⚛	🕊	🌐	🐇	ALERT
Baker's Blend	RJR	✓	✓	✓	No	?	✓	No	Yes*	?	✓	✗	cigarettes
Blue Bonnet	RJR	✓	✓	✓	No	?	✓	No	Yes*	?	✓	✗	cigarettes
Breakstone's	MO	✗	✓	✓	No	?	✓	No	Yes	?	✗	?	cigarettes

Company or Product	Abbr.	$	♀	✈	?	✈	⚛	🐄	🐾	🕊	ALERT
Chiffon	MO	✗	✓	No	?	✓	No	Yes	✗	?	cigarettes
Clear Brook	WF	?	?	No	?	✓	No	No	?	✗	
Country Crock	UN	✗	✓	No	✓*	✗	No	Yes†	?	?	
Countryside Spread	MO	✗	✓	No	?	✓	No	Yes	✗	?	cigarettes
Fleischmann's	RJR	✓	✓	No	✓*	?	No	Yes*	✗	?	cigarettes
Good Luck	UN	✗	✓	No	✓*	✗	No	Yes†	?	?	
Hotel Bar	BN	✗	✓	No	✓	✓	No	Yes†	?	✓	
Imperial	UN	✗	✓	No	✓*	✗	No	Yes†	?	?	
Keller's Butter	BN	✗	✓	No	✓	✓	No	Yes●	✓	✓	
Kraft	MO	✗	✓	No	?	✓	No	Yes	✗	?	cigarettes

✓ = Top Rating ✓ = Middle Rating ✗ = Bottom Rating ? = Insufficient Information
For a more detailed explanation see key on page 10

MARGARINE & BUTTER

MARGARINE & BUTTER

Company or Product	Abbr.	💲	♀	⚥	🏃	✈	🤝	⚛	🐰	☢	ALERT
Loriva #	LOR	?	?	?	✓	No	✗	No	?	✓	
Mazola	CPC	✗	✓	✓	✓	No	✓	No	✓	✓	
Parkay	MO	✗	✓	✓	?	No	✓	No	✗	?	cigarettes
Promise	UN	?	✓	?	✓*	No	✗	Yes†	?	?	
Protein-Aide #	LOR	?	✗	✓	✓	No	✗	No	?	✓	
Shedd's Spread	UN	✗	✓	✓	✓*	No	✗	Yes†	?	?	
Sun Valley	UN	✗	✓	✓	✓*	No	✗	Yes†	?	?	
Weight Watchers	HNZ	✓	?	✗	✓	No	✓	Yes	?	✓	dolphins caught
MEAT, CANNED											
Armour Star	G	?	✓	✓	✓	No	✓	No	✓	?	
Dinty Moore	HRL	✓	✓	✗	✓	No	✗	No	✓	✗	labor disputes
Fischer	WF	?	?	?	?	No	?	No	?	✗	

Company or Product	Abbr.	#	♀	✈	🐇	⚛	👥	🌐	ALERT
Hormel	HRL	✓	✓	No	✗	✓	✗	No	✗	labor disputes
Hunt's	BTC	✓+	✓	?	?	✓	?	No	✓	
Libby's	NEST	?	✓	No	?	?	✗	Yes†	✓	infant formula
Mary Kitchen	HRL	✓	✓	No	✗	✓	✗	No	✗	labor disputes
Masterpiece	WF	?	?	No	?	✓	?	No	✗	
John Morell	UB	✓	✓	No	✓	✗	?	No	✓	labor disputes
Not-So-Sloppy-Joe	HRL	✓	✓	No	✗	✓	✗	No	✗	labor disputes
SPAM	HRL	✓	✓	No	✗	✓	✗	No	✗	labor disputes
Swanson	CPB	✓	✓	No	✓	✓	✓	No	✓	on-site daycare
Underwood	WH	✓	✓	No	✓○	✓	✗	No	✓	

✓ = Top Rating ✓ = Middle Rating ✗ = Bottom Rating ? = Insufficient Information

For a more detailed explanation see key on page 10

MEAT, CANNED

MILK, CANNED AND EVAPORATED

Company or Product	Abbr.	$	⚥	✈	🏃	🐁	☢	🗺	🐬	🌐	ALERT
Alba	HNZ	✓	✓	No	✗	✓	No	Yes	✓	✓	dolphins caught
Carnation	NEST	?	?	No	?	✓	No	Yes†	?	✓	infant formula
Christopher's#	BARB	?	✓	No	✓	✓	No	No	✓	✗	
Coffee-Mate	BN	✗	✓	No	✓	✓	No	Yes●	✓	✓	
Coffeetwin	MO	✗	✓	No	✓	✓	No	Yes	✗	?	cigarettes
Cremora	BN	✗	✓	No	✓	✓	No	Yes●	?	✓	
Dairymate	WH	✓	✓	No	✓○	✗	No	No	?	✓	
Eagle Brand	BN	✗	✓	No	✓	✓	No	Yes●	✓	✓	
Kellogg's	K	✓	✓	No	?	✓	No	Yes●	✓	✓	
Knudsen	MO	✗	✓	No	?	✓	No	Yes	✗	?	cigarettes
Magnolia Brand	BN	✗	✓	No	✓	✓	No	Yes●	✓	✓	

Company or Product	Abbr.	💲	⚥	🧑	✈	🐇	⚛	⊕	👪	🌐	ALERT
Party Time	MO	✗	✓	✓	No	?	✓	No	Yes	?	cigarettes
Pet	WH	✓	✓	✓	No	✓○	✗	No	No	✓	
Sanalac	BTC	✓+	✓	?	No	?	?	No	No	✓	
ORAL HYGIENE											
Act	JNJ	✓	✓	✓	No	✓(*)	✓	No	Yes*	✓	
Aim	UN	✗	✓	✓	No	✓*	✓	No	Yes†	?	
Aquafresh	BECH	?	?	?	No	✗○	?	No	Yes†	?	
Aubrey Organics#	AUB	?	✓	✓	No	✓	✓	No	No	✓	
Avon	AVP	✓	✓	✓	No	✓(*)	✓	No	No	✓	
Cepacol	DOW	✓	✓	✓	No	✓(*)	✓	Yes	Yes	✓	makes pesticides

✓ = Top Rating   ✓ = Middle Rating   ✗ = Bottom Rating   ? = Insufficient Information

For a more detailed explanation see key on page 10

Page 153

ORAL HYGIENE

ORAL HYGIENE

Company or Product	Abbr.	$	♀	✈	(icon)	(icon)	⚛	(people)	(icon)	♻	ALERT
Clinomyn	CRCH	?	✓	?	✓*	✓	No	No	✓	✓	
Close-Up	UN	✗	✓	No	✓*	✓	No	Yes†	?	?	
Colgate	CL	✓+	✓	No	✓*	✗	No	Yes*	✓	✓	
Crest	PG	✓	✓	No	✓(*)	✓	No	Yes	✓	✓	disposable diapers
Dentagard	CL	✓+	✓	No	✓*	✓	No	Yes*	✓	✓	
Efferdent	WLA	✓	✓	No	✗○	✓	No	Yes●	✓	✓	disposable diapers
Fasteeth	PG	✓	✓	No	✓(*)	✓	No	Yes	✓	✓	disposable diapers
Fixodent	PG	✓	✓	No	✓(*)	✓	No	Yes	✓	✓	disposable diapers
Flourigard	CL	✓+	✓	No	✓*	✓	No	Yes*	✓	✓	
Gleem	PG	✓	✓	No	✓(*)	✓	No	Yes	✓	✓	disposable diapers
Listerine	WLA	✓	✓	No	✗○	✓	No	Yes●	✓	✓	
Listermint	WLA	✓	✓	No	✗○	✓	No	Yes●	✓	✓	

Company or Product	Abbr.	💲	♀	▨	✈	☼	▦	⚛	🐾	👪	♻	ALERT
Peak	CL	✓+	✓	✓	No	✓*	✓	✓	No	Yes*	✓	✓	
Pearl Drops	CAR	?	✗	?	No	✗○	?	✗	No	No	?	?	
Pepsodent	UN	✗	✓	✓	No	✓*	✗	✓	No	Yes†	?	?	
Prevent	JNJ	✓	✓	✓	No	✓(*)	✓	✓	No	Yes*	✓	✓	
Reach	JNJ	✓	✓	✗	No	✓(*)	✓	✓	No	Yes*	✓	✓	
Schiff	IBC	?	?	✓	No	✓	?	✗	No	No	?	✗	
Scope	PG	✓	✓	✗	No	✓(*)	✓	✓	No	Yes	✓	✓	disposable diapers
Signal	UN	✗	✓	✓	No	✓*	✓	✓	No	Yes†	?	?	
Tom's of Maine#	TOM	✓+	✗	✓	No	✓	✓	✓	No	No	✓	✓	
Ultra Brite	CL	✓+	✓	✓	No	✓*	✓	✓	No	Yes*	✓	✓	

✓ = Top Rating   ✓ = Middle Rating   ✗ = Bottom Rating   ? = Insufficient Information

For a more detailed explanation see key on page 10

ORAL HYGIENE

PAPER PRODUCTS

Company or Product	Abbr.	💲	⚥	✈	🤝	🐰	⚛	🌲	♻	ALERT
PAPER PRODUCTS										
Always	PG	✓	✓	No	✓(*)	✓	No	✓	✓	disposable diapers
Angel Soft	GP	?	✓	No	?	✓	No	✗	✗	clearcutting
Aurora	JR	✓	✗	No	?	✓	No	✗	✓	
Baby Fresh	SPP	✓	✓	No	✗	✓	No	✗	✓	forestry criticized
Baggies	MOB	?	✓	Yes	✓*	✓	No	✗	✓	
Basic	KMB	✗	?	No	?	✗	Yes●	✗	?	disposable diapers
Big 'n Thirsty	GP	?	✓	No	✓	✓	No	✗	✗	clearcutting
Blue Ribbon	JR	✓	✗	No	?	✓	No	✗	✓	
Bolt	JR	✓	✗	No	?	✓	No	✗	✓	
Bounty	PG	✓	✓	No	✓(*)	✓	Yes	✓	✓	disposable diapers
Brawny	JR	✓	✓	No	?	✓	No	✗	✓	

Company or Product	Abbr.	⚥	♀	🐾	✈	🤝	☢		🐾	🐇	ALERT
Carefree	JNJ	✓̃	✓	✓	No	✓	No	Yes*	✓	✓	
Charmin	PG	✓	✓	✓	No	✓	No	Yes	✓	✓	disposable diapers
Chubs	EK	✓	✓	✓	Yes	✓	No-	No	✓	✓	
Clout	KMB	✗	✓̃	✓̃	No	✗	No	Yes●	✗	?	disposable diapers
Coronet	MEA	✓	✓	✓̃	No	?	No	Yes	✓̃	✗	clearcutting
Coronet Sparkle	GP	?	✓̃	✓̃	No	✓	No	No	✗	✗	clearcutting
Cottonelle	SPP	✓̃	✓	✓	No	✓	No	No	✗	✓	forestry criticized
Cut-Rite	RLM	✗	✗	✗	No	✗	No	No	✗	✗	
Depend	KMB	✗	✓̃	✓̃	No	?	No	Yes●	✗	?	disposable diapers
Dixie	JR	✓̃	✓̃	✗	No.	✓̃	No	No	✗	✓̃	
											Page 157

✓ = Top Rating ✓̃ = Middle Rating ✗ = Bottom Rating ? = Insufficient Information

For a more detailed explanation see key on page 10

PAPER PRODUCTS

Company or Product	Abbr.	💲	♀+	🧴	✈	🤖	🐾	⚛	♻	🌼	ALERT
Gartex	JR	✓	✓	✗	No	✓	✓	No	No	✗	
Georgia-Pacific	GP	?	✓	?	No	✓	✓	No	No	✗	clearcutting
Glad	FB	?	?	?	No	✓	?	No	?	✗	
Handi-Wrap	DOW	✓	✓	✓	No	✓(*)	✓	Yes	✓	✓	makes pesticides
Handi Wipes	CL	✓+	✓	✓	No	✓*	✓	No	Yes*	✓	
Hefty	MOB	?	✓	✓	Yes	✓*	✓	No	✗	✓	
Hi-Dri	KMB	✗	✓	✓	No	?	✗	Yes●	✗	?	disposable diapers
Huggies	KMB	✗	✓	✓	No	?	✗	Yes●	✗	?	disposable diapers
Johnson's	JNJ	✓	✓	✓	No	✓(*)	✓	Yes*	✓	✓	
Kleenex	KMB	✗	✓	✓	No	?	✗	Yes●	✗	?	disposable diapers
Kotex	KMB	✗	✓	✓	No	?	✗	Yes●	✗	?	disposable diapers
Lehn & Fink	EK	✓	✓	✓	Yes	✓(*)	✓	No	✓	✓	

Company or Product	Abbr.	💲	⚥	✈	🐾	🔬	⚛	👥	🌐	ALERT
Lightdays	KMB	✗	✓	No	✓	?	No	Yes●	✗	?	disposable diapers
Luvs	PG	✓	✓	No	✓	✓(*)	No	Yes	✓	✓	disposable diapers
Mead	MEA	✓	✓	No	✓	?	No	Yes	✓	✗	clearcutting
Natural Touch	JR	✓	✗	No	✗	?	No	No	✗	✓	
New Freedom	KMB	✗	✓	No	✗	?	No	Yes●	✗	?	disposable diapers
Nice 'n Soft	JR	✓	✓	No	✗	?	No	No	✓	✓	
Northern	JR	✓	✓	No	✗	?	No	No	✓	✗	
o.b.	JNJ	✓	✓	No	✓	✓(*)	No	Yes*	✓	✗	
Pampers	PG	✓	✓	No	✓	✓(*)	No	Yes	✓	✓	disposable diapers
Proline	BN	✗	✓	No	✓	✓	No	Yes●	✓	✓	

✓ = Top Rating   ✓ = Middle Rating   ✗ = Bottom Rating   ? = Insufficient Information

For a more detailed explanation see key on page 10

PAPER PRODUCTS

Company or Product	Abbr.	$	♀	(icon)	(icon)	(icon)	(icon)	⚛	(icon)	(icon)	ALERT
Puffs	PG	✓	✓	✓	No	✓(*)	✓	No	Yes	✓	disposable diapers
Q-Tips	UN	✗	✓	✗	No	✓*	✓	No	Yes†	?	
Reynold's	RLM	✗	✗	✗	No	✓	✓	No	No	✗	
Reynold's Wrap	RLM	✗	✗	✗	No	✓	✓	No	No	✗	
Saran Wrap	DOW	✓	✓	✓	No	✓(*)	✓	Yes	Yes	✓	makes pesticides
Scott	SPP	✓	✓	✓	No	✗	✓	No	No	✓	forestry criticized
Scotties	SPP	✓	✓	✓	No	✗	✓	No	No	✓	forestry criticized
ScotTowels	SPP	✓	✓	✓	No	✗	✓	No	No	✓	forestry criticized
Security	KMB	✗	✓	✗	No	?	✗	No	Yes●	?	disposable diapers
Serenity	JNJ	✓	✓	✓	No	✗	✓	No	Yes*	✓	
Simplique	KMB	✗	✓	✗	No	?	✗	No	Yes●	?	disposable diapers
Softex	GP	?	✓	✓	No	✓	✓	No	No	✗	clearcutting

PAPER PRODUCTS

Company or Product	Abbr.	💲	♀	(icon)	(icon)	(icon)	(icon)	⚛	(icon)	(icon)	(icon)	ALERT
Softique	KMB	✖	✓	✓	No	?	✖	No	Yes●	✖	✓	?	disposable diapers
Sparkle	GP	?	✓	✖	No	✓	✓	No	No	✖	✖	✖	clearcutting
Spill-Mate	JR	✓	✓	✖	No	?	✓	No	No	✓	✖	✓	
Stayfree	JNJ	✓	✓	✓	No	✓(●)	✓	No	Yes*	✓	✓	✓	
Sure & Natural	JNJ	✓	✓	✓	No	✓(●)	✓	No	Yes*	✓	✓	✓	
Tuff-N-Tidy	GP	?	✓	✖	No	?	✓	No	No	✖	✖	✖	clearcutting
Vanity Fair	JR	✓	✓	✓	No	✖	✖	No	No	✖	✓	✓	
Viva	SPP	✓	✓	✓	No	✖	✓	No	No	✓	✖	✓	forestry criticized
Wet Ones	EK	✓	✓	✓	Yes	✓(●)	✓	No	No	✖	✓	✓	
Zee	JR	✓	✓	✖	No	?	✓	No	No	✖	✖	✓	

✓ = Top Rating   ✔ = Middle Rating   ✖ = Bottom Rating   ? = Insufficient Information

For a more detailed explanation see key on page 10

Company or Product	Abbr.	💲	♀	⚗	🕊	⚛			✿	ALERT
Ziploc	DOW	✓	✓	✓	No	✓	Yes	Yes	✓	makes pesticides
PASTA AND RICE										
Anthony's	BN	✗	✓	✓	No	✓	No	No	✓	
Arrowhead Mills#	AM	?	✓	?	No	✓	No	No	✓	
Betty Crocker	GIS	✓+	✓	✓	No	✓	No	No	✓	
Bimco	BN	✗	✓	✓	No	✓	No	Yes●	✓	
Borden	BN	✗	✓	✓	No	✓	No	Yes●	✓	
Bravo	BN	✗	✓	✓	No	✓	No	Yes●	✓	
Chef's Series	CPC	✗	✓	✓	No	✓	No	No	✓	
Creamette Brand	BN	✗	✓	✓	No	✓	No	Yes●	✓	
Dutch Maid	BN	✗	✓	✓	No	✓	No	Yes●	✓	
Eden#	EDEN	✗	✗	✓	No	✓	No	No	✗	

Company or Product	Abbr.										ALERT
El Molino#	AMH	?	✓	✓	No	✓	✓	No	?	✗	
Falcon Trading#	FALC	?	✗	✓	No	✓	✓	No	✓	✓	
General Foods	MO	✗	✓	✓	No	?	✓	Yes	✗	?	cigarettes
Gioia	BN	✗	✓	✓	No	✓	✓	Yes●	✓	✓	
Globe A-1	BN	✗	✓	✓	No	✓	✓	Yes●	✓	✓	
Gold Medal	HSY	✓	✓	✓	No	?	✓	No	✓	✓	
Golden Grain	OAT	✓	✓	✓	No	✓	✓	No	✓	✓	
Gooch Foods	ADM	?	?	?	No	?	✓	No	✓	✗	
Goodman's	BN	✗	✓	✓	No	✓	✓	Yes●	✓	✓	
Health Valley Nat. Foods#	HVAL	?	✓	✓	No	?	✓	No	✓	✗	

✓ = Top Rating   ⟋ = Middle Rating   ✗ = Bottom Rating   ? = Insufficient Information
For a more detailed explanation see key on page 10.

PASTA AND RICE

Company or Product	Abbr.	💲	⚥	✈	🕊	🌍	⚛	🐾	♻	ALERT
Herb's Homestyle Pasta#	EDEN	✗	✗	No	✓	✓	No	✓	No	✗	
Homestyle	BN	✗	✓	No	✓	✓	No	✓	Yes●	✓	
Kraft	MO	✗	✓	No	?	✓	No	✗	Yes	?	cigarettes
La Rosa	ADM	?	✓	No	✓	?	No	✓	No	✗	
Lipton	UN	✗	✓	No	✓*	✗	No	?	Yes†	?	
Luxury Merlino's	BN	✗	✓	No	✓	✓	No	✓	Yes●	✓	
Macaroni & Cheese	MO	✗	✓	No	?	✓	No	✗	Yes	?	cigarettes
Martha Gooch	ADM	?	✓	No	?	?	No	✓	No	✗	
Mrs. Grass	BN	✗	✓	No	✓	✓	No	✓	Yes●	✓	
Mueller's	CPC	✗	✓	No	✓	✓	No	✓	No	✓	
New Mill	BN	✗	✓	No	✓	✓	No	✓	Yes●	✓	
Pennsylvania Dutch	BN	✗	✓	No	✓	✓	No	✓	Yes●	✓	

Company or Product	Abbr.	💲	⊕	✈	👪	⚛	🌸		ALERT
Prince	BN	✗	✔	✔	No	✔	✔	No	Yes●	✔	
R&F	BN	✗	✔	✔	No	✔	✔	No	Yes●	✔	
Red Cross	BN	✗	✔	✔	No	✔	✔	No	Yes●	✔	
Rice-A-Roni	OAT	✔	✔	✔	No	✔	✔	No	No	✔	
Ronco	BN	✗	✔	✔	No	✔	✔	No	Yes●	✔	
Ronzoni	MO	?	✔	✔	No	✔	✔	No	Yes	?	cigarettes
Russo	ADM	?	?	✔	No	?	?	No	No	✗	
San Giorgio	HSY	✔	✔	✔	No	✔	✔	No	✔	✔	
Suddenly Salad	GIS	✔+	✔	✔	No	✔	✔	No	✔	✔	
Suzy Wan	MO	✗	✔	✔	No	✔	✔	No	Yes	?	cigarettes

✔ = Top Rating   ✓ = Middle Rating   ✗ = Bottom Rating   ? = Insufficient Information
For a more detailed explanation see key on page 10

PASTA AND RICE

PET FOOD AND PET PRODUCTS

Company or Product	Abbr.	$	♀+	▨	✈	✍	✊	⚛	🐾	✡	ALERT
Sweet Cloud#	GES	?	✓	✓	No	✓	✗	No	✓	✗	
Uncle Ben's	MARS	?	?	?	No	?	?	No	?	?	
Zen Mountain#	GES	?	✓	✓	No	✓	✗	No	✓	✗	

PET FOOD AND PET PRODUCTS

Company or Product	Abbr.	$	♀+	▨	✈	✍	✊	⚛	🐾	✡	ALERT
9 Lives	HNZ	✓	✓	✗	No	✓	✓	No	✓	✓	dolphins caught
Alley Kat	RAL	✗	✓	✗	No	✓	✗	No	✓	✗	dolphins caught
Amore	HNZ	✓	✓	✗	No	✓	✓	No	✓	✓	dolphins caught
Bonz	RAL	✗	✓	✗	No	✓	✗	No	✓	✗	dolphins caught
Bright Eyes	NEST	?	?	?	No	?	✗	Yes†	?	✓	infant formula
Bumble Bee	GMP	?	?	?	No	?	?	Yes†	?	?	dolphins caught
Carnation	NEST	?	?	?	No	?	✗	Yes†	?	✓	infant formula
Chef's Blend	CLX	✓	✓	✓	No	✓*	✓	No	✓	✓	

Company or Product	Abbr.	$	[icon]	[icon]	[icon]	[icon]	[icon]	[icon]	[icon]	[icon]	ALERT
Chuck Wagon	RAL	✖	✓	No	✓	✓	No	No	✓	✖	dolphins caught
Come N Get It	NEST	?	?	No	?	?	No	Yes†	✓	✓	infant formula
Fancy Feast	NEST	?	?	No	?	?	No	Yes†	✓	✓	infant formula
Figaro	GMP	?	✓	No	?	?	?	Yes†	?	?	dolphins caught
Fresh Step	CLX	✓	✓	No	✓*	✓	No	No	✓	✓	
Friskies	NEST	?	?	No	?	?	No	Yes†	✓	✓	infant formula
Grand Gourmet	NEST	?	?	No	?	?	No	Yes†	✓	✓	infant formula
Jerky	HNZ	✓	✓	No	✖	✓	No	Yes	✓	✓	dolphins caught
Ken-L Ration	OAT	✓	✓	No	✓	✓	No	No	✓	✓	
Kibbles 'N Bits	OAT	✓	✓	No	✓	✓	No	No	✓	✓	

✓ = Top Rating   ✓ = Middle Rating   ✖ = Bottom Rating   ? = Insufficient Information

For a more detailed explanation see key on page 10

PET FOOD AND PET PRODUCTS

Company or Product	Abbr.	$	♀					⚛			ALERT
King Kuts	OAT	✓	✓	✓	No	✓	✓	No	✓	✓	
Kit 'N Kaboodle	RAL	✗	✓	✗	No	✓	✓	No	✓	✗	dolphins caught
Litter Green	CLX	✓	✓	✓	No	✓*	✓	No	✓	✓	
Meaty Bone	HNZ	✓	✓	✗	No	✓	✓	Yes	✓	✓	dolphins caught
Meow Mix	RAL	✗	✓	✗	No	✓	✓	No	✗	✗	dolphins caught
Mighty Dog	NEST	?	?	?	No	?	✗	Yes†	?	✓	infant formula
Milk Bone	RJR	✓	✓	✓	No	✓	?	Yes*	✓	✗	cigarettes
Organimals#	AUB	?	✓	✓	No	✓	✓	No	✓	✓	
Pounce	OAT	✓	✓	✓	No	✓	✓	No	✓	✓	
Purina	RAL	✗	✓	✗	No	✓	✓	No	✗	✗	dolphins caught
Ralston	RAL	✗	✓	✗	No	✓	✓	No	✗	✗	dolphins caught
Recipe	HNZ	✓	✓	✗	No	✓	✓	No	Yes	✓	dolphins caught

Company or Product	Abbr.	💲	⚥					⚛				ALERT
StarKist	HNZ	✔	✔	✗	No	✔	✔	No	Yes	✔	✔	dolphins caught
Tender Vittles	RAL	✗	✗	✗	No	✔	✔	No	No	✔	✗	dolphins caught
Universal Labs#	ULAB	?	✔	?	No	?	✔	No	No	✔	✗	
PREPARED FOODS												
21st Century Foods#	TFC	✗	✔	✔	No	✔	✔	No	No	✔	✔	
American Home Foods	AHP	✗	✗	✗	No	✔(*)	✔○	No	Yes*	✗	✔	✗	infant formula
B & M	WH	✔	✔	✔	No	✔	✔	No	No	✗	✔	
Betty Crocker	GIS	✔+	✔	✔	No	✔	✔	No	No	✔	✔	
Burrito Grande	HRL	✔	✔	✗	No	✔	✔	No	No	✗	✔	labor disputes
Campbell's	CPB	✔	✔	✔	No	✔	?	No	No	✔	✔	on-site daycare

✔ = Top Rating   ✓ = Middle Rating   ✗ = Bottom Rating   ? = Insufficient Information

For a more detailed explanation see key on page 10

PREPARED FOODS

Company or Product	Abbr.	$	O+	(minorities)	(military)	(animal testing)	(disarmament)	(nuclear) ⚛	(environment)	(misc)	ALERT
Chef Boyardee	AHP	✗	✓	✗	No	✓(*)	✓	✓	No	Yes*	✗	infant formula
Chi-Chi's	HRL	✓	✓	✗	No	✓	✓	✗	No	No	✗	labor disputes
Contadina	NEST	?	?	?	No	✓	✓	✗	No	Yes†	✓	infant formula
Country Store	BN	✗	✓	✓	No	✓	✓	✓	No	Yes●	✓	
Franco-American	CPB	✓	✓	✓	No	?	✓	✓	No	No	✓	on-site daycare
Health Valley Nat. Foods#	HVAL	?	?	✓	No	?	?	?	No	No	✗	
Heinz	HNZ	✓	✓	✗	No	✓	✓	✓	No	Yes	✓	dolphins caught
Homestyle#	HOME	?	?	✗	No	?	?	?	No	No	?	
Hormel	HRL	✓	✓	✗	No	✓	✓	✗	No	No	✗	labor disputes
Hungry Jack	GMP	?	?	?	No	✓	✓	?	?	Yes†	✓	dolphins caught
La Choy	BTC	✓+	✓	✓	No	?	✓	?	No	No	✓	
Lifetone International#	LFTI	?	✗	✗	No	?	✗	✗	?	No	✓	

Company or Product	Abbr.	💲	♀	〘 ⬤	⬛	—	🏃	✋	⚛	🔬	✖	ALERT
Loma Linda	LOMA	?	✓	✓	No	✓	✓	✗	No	✓	✗	
Mama Leone's	AHP	✗	✓	✗	No	✓(*)	✓	✓	Yes*	✓	✗	infant formula
Millstone	LOMA	?	✓	✓	No	✓	✓	✗	No	✓	✗	
Old El Paso	WH	✓	✓	✓	No	✓○	?	✗	No	?	✓	
Oriental Classics	GIS	✓+	✓	✓	No	✓	✓	✓	No	✓	✓	
Ortega	RJR	✓	✓	✗	No	✓	✓	?	Yes*	✗	✗	cigarettes
Pacific Garden#	ACOP	?	✓	✓	No	✓○	✓	✓	No	✓	✓	
Pancho Villa	WH	✓	✓	✓	No	✗	✗	✗	No	?	✓	
Pillsbury	GMP	?	?	?	?	?	?	?	Yes†	?	?	dolphins caught
Potato Buds	GIS	✓+	✓	✓	No	✓	✓	✓	No	✓	✓	

✓ = Top Rating ✓ = Middle Rating ✗ = Bottom Rating ? = Insufficient Information
For a more detailed explanation see key on page 10

PREPARED FOODS

Company or Product	Abbr.	💲	⚥	🌐	✈🌲	🐰	⚖	♻	⚛	🐾	⬡	ALERT
Progresso Mexican Food	WH	✓	✓	✓	No	✓○	✓	✗	No	?	✓	
Roger's Foods	UFC	✓	✓	✗	No	✓	✓	✓	No	?	?	
Suzi Wan	MARS	?	?	?	No	✓	✗	?	No	?	?	
Uncle Ben's	MARS	?	?	?	No	✗	✗	?	No	?	?	
Van Camps	OAT	✓	✓	✓	No	✓	✓	✓	No	✓	✓	
Vegetarian Health#	VH	?	?	?	No	✓	✓	?	No	?	?	
PROPRIETARY REMEDIES												
4-Way Nasal Spray	BMY	✓	✓	?	No	✓(*)	✓	✓	Yes*	?	✗	infant formula
Advil	AHP	✗	✓	✗	No	✓(*)	✓	✗	Yes*	?	✗	infant formula
Afrin	SGP	✓	✓	✓	No	✓(*)	✓	✓	Yes●	✓	✓	
Alka-Seltzer	MILS	?	?	✓	No	✗○	✓	✓	Yes†	?	✗	
America's Home Remedy	MILS	?	?	?	No	✗○	✓	?	Yes†	?	✗	

Company or Product	Abbr.	💲	⚥	✦	✈	◈	⚛	✧	✸	ALERT
American Health#	AMH	?	✓	✓	No	✓	✗	No	No	?	
Ammens	BMY	✓	✓	✓	No	✓(*)	✓	No	Yes*	?	infant formula
Anacin	AHP	✗	✗	✓	No	✓(*)	✓	No	Yes*	✓	infant formula
Anbesol	AHP	✗	✗	✓	No	✓(*)	✓	No	Yes*	✓	infant formula
Anusol	WLA	✓	✓	✓	No	✗○	✓	No	Yes●	✓	
Ascriptin	ROR	?	✗	✓	No	✗○	✓	No	No	?	
Bactidol	WLA	✓	✓	✓	No	✗○	✓	No	Yes●	✓	
Bayer	EK	✓	✓	✓	Yes	✓(*)	✓	No	No	✓	
Ben Gay	PFE	✓	✓	✓	No	✓(*)	✓	No	Yes●	✗	heart-valve suit
Benadryl	WLA	✓	✓	✓	No	✗●	✓	No	Yes●	✓	

✓ = Top Rating   ✓ = Middle Rating   ✗ = Bottom Rating   ? = Insufficient Information
For a more detailed explanation see key on page 10

PROPRIETARY REMEDIES

PROPRIETARY REMEDIES

Company or Product	Abbr.	$	⚥	[icon 3]	[icon 4]	[icon 5]	[icon 6]	[icon 7]	⚛	[icon 9]	[icon 10]	[icon 11]	ALERT
Benylin	WLA	✓	✓	✓	No	✗	✓	✓	No	Yes●	✓	✓	
Bromo-Seltzer	WLA	✓	✓	✓	No	✗	✓	✓	No	Yes●	✓	✓	
Bufferin	BMY	✓	✓	✓	No	✓*	?	?	No	Yes*	?	✗	infant formula
Bugs Bunny Vitamins	MILS	?	?	?	No	✗	?	?	No	Yes†	?	✗	
Caladryl	WLA	✓	✓	✓	No	✗	✓	✓	No	Yes●	✓	✓	
Centrum	ACY	✓	✓	✓	No	✗	?	✓	No	Yes*	✗	✓	makes pesticides
Cepacol	DOW	✓	✓	✓	No	✓*	✓	✓	Yes	Yes	✓	✓	makes pesticides
Cheracol	UPJ	✓	✗	✓	No	✗	✓	✓	No	Yes●	✓	✓	
Clear Eyes	ABT	✗	✓	?	No	✗	✓	✓	No	Yes*	✓	✓	infant formula
Comtrex	BMY	✓	✓	✓	No	✓*	✓	✓	No	Yes●	?	✗	infant formula
Coricidin	SGP	✓	✓	✓	No	✓*	✓	✓	No	Yes●	✓	✓	
Correctol	SGP	✓	✓	✓	No	✓*	✓	✓	No	Yes●	✓	✓	

Company or Product	Abbr.	$	⚥										ALERT
Datril	BMY	✓	✓	✓	No	✓(*)	✓	✓	No	Yes*	?	✗	infant formula
Deer Valley#	DVF	✗	✓	✗	No	✓	✓	?	No	No	✓	✗	
Dristan	AHP	✗	✓	✗	No	✓(*)	✓	✓	No	Yes*	✓	✗	infant formula
Drixoral	SGP	✓	✓	✓	No	✓(*)	✓	✓	No	Yes●	✓	✓	
Duration	SGP	✓	✓	✓	No	✓(*)	✓	✓	No	Yes●	✓	✓	
Feldene	PFE	✓	✓	✓	No	✓(*)	✓	✓	No	Yes*	✓	✗	heart-valve suit
Fiber Con	ACY	✓	✓	?	No	✗○	✓	?	No	Yes*	✗	✓	makes pesticides
Fibre Trim	SGP	✓	✓	✓	No	✓(*)	✓	✓	No	Yes●	✓	✓	
Flintstones Vitamins	MILS	?	?	?	No	✗○	✓	?	No	Yes†●	?	✗	
Gelusil	WLA	✓	✓	✓	No	✗○	✓	✓	No	Yes●	✓	✓	

✓ = Top Rating   ✓ = Middle Rating   ✗ = Bottom Rating   ? = Insufficient Information

For a more detailed explanation see key on page 10

PROPRIETARY REMEDIES

Page 175

Company or Product	Abbr.	$	♀	(icon)	✈	(icon)	(icon)	(icon)	⚛	(icon)	(icon)	ALERT
Hall's	WLA	✓	✓	✓	No	✗○	✓	✓	No	Yes●	✓	
Head & Chest	PG	✓	✓	✓	No	✓(*)	✓	✓	No	Yes	✓	disposable diapers
Kaopectate	UPJ	✓	✓	✓	No	✗○	✓	✓	No	Yes●	✓	
Luden's	HSY	✓	✓	✓	No	?	✓	✓	No	No	✓	
Maalox	ROR	?	✓	✗	No	✗○	✓	✓	No	No	?	
McNeil	JNJ	✓	✓	✓	No	✓(●)	✓	✓	No	Yes*	✓	
Mead Johnson & Co.	BMY	✓	✓	✓	No	✓(*)	✓	✓	No	Yes*	?	infant formula
Medipren	JNJ	✓	✓	✓	No	✓(*)	✓	✓	No	Yes*	✓	
Metamucil	PG	✓	✓	✓	No	✓(*)	✓	✓	No	Yes	✓	disposable diapers
Momentum	AHP	✗	✓	✗	No	✓(*)	✓	✓	No	Yes*	?	infant formula
Motrin	UPJ	✓	✓	✓	No	✗○	✓	✓	No	Yes●	✓	
Murine	ABT	✗	✗	?	No	✗○	✓	✓	No	Yes●	✓	infant formula

Company or Product	Abbr.	#	♀				⚛			ALERT
Myadec	WLA	✓	✓	No	✗○	✓	No	Yes●	✓	✓	
N'ICE	BECH	?	?	No	✗○	✓	No	Yes†	?	✓	
Naturalax#	MUR	?	✓	No	✓	✓	No	No	?	✓	
Nature's Herbs#	HERB	?	✗	No	✓	✗	No	No	?	?	
Nature's Way#	MUR	?	✓	No	✓	✓	No	No	✓	✓	
NEO-Synephrine	EK	✓	✓	Yes	✓(*)	✓	No	No	✓	✓	
No-Doz	BMY	✓	✓	No	✓(*)	✓	No	Yes*	?	✗	infant formula
Ocuclear	SGP	✓	✓	No	✓(*)	✓	No	Yes●	✓	✓	
One-A-Day	MILS	?	?	No	✗○	✓	No	Yes†	?	✗	
Origin#	AMH	?	✓	No	✓	✓	No	No	?	✗	

✓ = Top Rating   ◌ = Middle Rating   ✗ = Bottom Rating   ? = Insufficient Information

For a more detailed explanation see key on page 10

PROPRIETARY REMEDIES

Company or Product	Abbr.	💲	⚥	🏳	✈	🐾	♻	⚛	🌐	🌍	ALERT
Panadol	EK	✓	✓	✓	Yes	✓(*)	✓	No	✓	✓	
Pepto-Bismol	PG	✓	✓	✓	No	✓(*)	✓	No	✓	✓	disposable diapers
Phillips	EK	✓	✓	✓	Yes	✓(*)	✓	No	✓	✓	
Poly Vi-Sol Vitamins	BMY	✓	✗	✓	No	✓(*)	✓	Yes*	?	✗	infant formula
Preparation H	AHP	✗	✓	✗	No	✓(*)	✓	Yes*	✓	✗	infant formula
Primatene	AHP	✗	✓	✗	No	✓(*)	✗	Yes*	✓	✗	infant formula
Radiance#	AMH	?	✓	✓	No	✓	✓	No	?	✗	
Remegel	WLA	✓	✓	✓	No	✗○	✗	Yes●	?	✓	
Resolve	DOW	✓	✓	✓	No	✓(*)	✓	Yes	✓	✓	makes pesticides
Rolaids	WLA	✓	✓	✓	No	✗○	✓	Yes●	✓	✓	
Schiff	IBC	?	✓	✗	No	✓	?	No	?	✗	
Sine-Aid	JNJ	✓	✓	✓	No	✓(*)	✓	Yes*	✓	✓	

Company or Product	Abbr.	$	♀				⚛			ALERT
Sinutab	WLA	✓	✓	No	✗○	✓	No	Yes●	✓	
Sleep-Eze	AHP	✗	✗	No	✓(*)	✗	No	Yes*	✗	infant formula
Solgar Company	SLGR	?	?	No	?	?	No	?	?	
Sominex	BECH	?	?	No	?	?	No	Yes†	✓	
St. Joseph's	SGP	✓	✓	No	✓(*)	✓	No	Yes●	✓	
Stressgard	MILS	?	?	No	✗○	?	No	Yes†	✗	
Sucrets	BECH	?	?	No	✗	?	No	Yes†	✓	
Theracal	WLA	✓	✓	No	✗○	✓	No	Yes●	✓	
Theragran-M	SQB	?	✓	No	✗○	✓	No	Yes●	?	
Trendar	AHP	✗	✗	No	✓(*)	✗	No	Yes*	✗	infant formula

✓ = Top Rating   ✓ = Middle Rating   ✗ = Bottom Rating   ? = Insufficient Information
For a more detailed explanation see key on page 10

PROPRIETARY REMEDIES

Page 179

PROPRIETARY REMEDIES

Company or Product	Abbr.	$	♀⚲		✈ -				⚛		ALERT
Tronolane	ABT	✗	✓	?	No	✗○	✓	✓	Yes●	✓	infant formula
Tucks	WLA	✓	✓	✓	No	✗○	✓	✓	Yes●	✓	
Twin Labs	TWIN	?	✓	✓	No	✓	✓	?	No	✗	
Tylenol	JNJ	✓	✓	✓	No	✓(*)	✗	✓	Yes*	✓	
Unicap	UPJ	✓	✓	✓	No	✗○	✓	✓	Yes●	✓	
Unisom	PFE	✓	✓	✓	No	✓(*)	✓	✓	Yes●	✗	heart-valve suit
Universal Labs#	ULAB	?	✓	?	No	✓	?	✓	No	✗	
Vanquish	EK	✓	✓	✓	Yes	✓(*)	✓	✓	Yes	✓	
Vicks Formula 44	PG	✓	✓	✓	No	✓(*)	✓	✓	Yes	✓	disposable diapers
Vicks Vaporub	PG	✓	✓	✓	No	✓(*)	✓	✓	Yes	✓	disposable diapers
Visene	PFE	✓	✓	✓	No	✓(*)	✓	✓	Yes●	✗	heart-valve suit
Vital Life#	KLAB	?	✓	?	No	✓	✗	✓	No	✗	

Company or Product	Abbr.	💲	⚥	[icon]	[icon]	⚛	[icon]	[icon]	[icon]	ALERT
Vivarin	BECH	?	?	?	No	Yes†	No	?	✓	
Whitehall Laboratories	AHP	✗	✓	✗	No	Yes*	No	✓	✗	infant formula
REFRIGERATED & FROZEN DESSERTS										
Ben & Jerry's	B&J	✓+	✓	✗○	No	No	No	✓	✓	1% for peace
Bird's Eye	MO	✗	✓	?	No	Yes	No	✓	?	cigarettes
Bon Bons	NEST	?	?	?	No	Yes†	No	✓	✓	infant formula
Borden	BN	✗	✓	✓	No	Yes●	No	✗	✓	
Breyer's	MO	✗	✓	✓	No	Yes	No	✓	?	cigarettes
Casera	CPB	✓	✓	?	No	No	No	✓	✓	on-site daycare
Chiquita	UB	✓	✓	✓	No	No	No	✗	✓	labor disputes

✓ = Top Rating ✓ = Middle Rating ✗ = Bottom Rating ? = Insufficient Information

For a more detailed explanation see key on page 10

Page 181

REFRIGERATED & FROZEN DESSERTS

REFRIGERATED & FROZEN DESSERTS

Company or Product	Abbr.	💲	♀	👥	✈	🏃	🐾	⚛	🐟	🐱	ALERT
Cream Tops#	HOME	?	✗	✗	No	✓	?	No	No	✓	
Crystal Light	MO	✗	✓	✓	No	?	✓	No	Yes	✗	cigarettes
Dean	DF	?	✓	?	No	?	✗	No	No	✗	
Foremost	MO	✗	✓	✓	No	?	✓	No	Yes	?	cigarettes
Frostee	BN	✗	✓	✓	No	✓*	✓	No	Yes●	✓	
Fruit-Line	UN	✗	✓	✓	No	✓	✗	No	Yes†	?	
Fruit Tops#	HOME	?	✗	✗	No	?	?	No	No	✓	
Fruit 'n Juice	CKE	?	✗	?	No	?	✗	No	No	✓	pesticide use
Frusen Gladje	MO	✗	✓	✓	No	?	✓	No	Yes	?	cigarettes
Gelare	BN	✗	✓	✓	No	✓	✓	No	Yes●	✓	
Gold Rush	GIS	✓+	✓	✓	No	✓	✓	No	No	✓	
Gone Bananas#	IF	?	✓	✗	No	✓	✓	No	No	✗	

Company or Product	Abbr.	💲	♀		🤝	🌲	🐇	⚛		🕊	ALERT
Good Humor	UN	✗	✓	✓	✗	✓	✓*	No	Yes†	?	?	
Häagen-Dazs	GMP	?	?	?	?	✗	?	No	Yes†	?	?	dolphins caught
Heaven	NEST	?	?	✓	✗	✓	?	No	Yes†	✓	✓	infant formula
Homestyle#	HOME	?	✗	✗	?	✓	?	No	No	✓	✓	
Jell-O	MO	✗	✓	✓	✓	✓	?	No	Yes	✗	?	cigarettes
Louis Sherry	BN	✗	✓	✗	✓	✓	✓	No	Yes●	✓	✓	
Meadow Gold	BN	✗	✓	✗	✓	✓	✓	No	Yes●	✓	✓	
Minimilk	UN	✗	✓	✓	✗	✓	✓*	No	Yes†	?	?	
Mrs. Smith's	K	✓	✓	✓	✓	✓	?	No	Yes●	✓	✓	
Nabisco	RJR	✓	✓	✓	✗	✓	?	No	Yes*	✗	✗	cigarettes

✓ = Top Rating ✗ = Bottom Rating ✓ = Middle Rating ? = Insufficient Information

For a more detailed explanation see key on page 10

Page 183

REFRIGERATED & FROZEN DESSERTS

REFRIGERATED & FROZEN DESSERTS

Company or Product	Abbr.	💲	♀	〰	✈	🐰	🎿	⚛	🐾	🕊	ALERT
Nestle	NEST	?	?	?	No	?	✓	No	?	✓	infant formula
Nice 'n Light	MO	✗	✓	✓	No	?	✓	Yes	✗	?	cigarettes
Pepperidge Farm	CPB	✓	✓	✓	No	?	✓	No	✗	✓	on-site daycare
Polar B'ar	MO	✗	✓	✓	No	?	✓	Yes	✗	?	cigarettes
Rice Dream#	IF	?	✓	✗	No	✓	✓	No	✓	✗	
Sara Lee	SLE	✓	✓	✓	No	✓	✓	Yes	✓	✓	
Sealtest	MO	✗	✓	✓	No	?	✓	Yes	✗	?	cigarettes
Stater Bros.	MO	✗	✓	✓	No	?	✓	Yes	✗	?	cigarettes
Stillwell	FLO	?	✗	?	No	?	✓	No	?	✗	
Sunkist	UN	✗	✓	✓	No	✓*	✓	Yes†	?	?	
Tillamook Cheese	TILA	✗	✓	✓	No	?	✗	No	✓	✗	
Toll House	NEST	?	?	?	No	?	✗	Yes†	?	✓	infant formula

Company or Product	Abbr.	#	♀						⚛			ALERT
Weight Watchers	HNZ	✔	✓	✘	No	✔	✓	No	Yes	✓	✓	dolphins caught
White Rose	DIG	?	?	?	No	?	✓	No	No	✓	✘	
REFRIGERATED MEATS												
Armour	CAG	?	✓	?	No	?	✘	✓	No	✓	?	OSHA fines
Bob Ostrow	Ub	✓	✓	✓	No	✓	✘	✓	No	?	✓	labor disputes
Buckboard	UB	✓	✓	✓	No	✔	✘	✓	No	?	✓	labor disputes
Carando	DIG	?	✓	?	No	?	✓	✓	No	?	✘	
Cobblestone Mill	FLO	?	✘	?	No	✓	✓	✓	No	?	✘	
Cornish	TYSN	?	✓	✘	No	✓	✘	✓	No	?	✘	labor disputes
E-Z Cut	UB	✓	✓	✓	No	✓	✘	✓	No	?	✓	labor disputes

✔ = Top Rating   ✓ = Middle Rating   ✘ = Bottom Rating   ? = Insufficient Information
For a more detailed explanation see key on page 10

REFRIGERATED MEATS

Company or Product	Abbr.	💲	⚥	〰️	✈️	🐇	🌐	⚛️	👪	🌍	ALERT
Gold Leaf	HFF	?	✗	?	No	?	?	No	✗	?	
Golden Smoked	UB	✓	✓	✓	No	✓	✗	No	?	✓	labor disputes
Health Valley Nat. Foods#	HVAL	?	✓	✓	No	?	?	No	✓	✗	
Hillshire Farm	SLE	✓	✓	✓	No	✓	✓	Yes	✓	✓	
Holly Farms	HFF	?	✗	?	No	✗	?	No	✗	?	
Hormel	HRL	✓	✓	✗	No	✓	✗	No	✗	✗	labor disputes
Hunter	UB	✓	✓	✓	No	✓	✗	No	?	✓	labor disputes
Jesse Jones	GIS	✓+	✓	✓	No	✓	✓	No	✓	✓	
John Morrell	UB	✓	✓	✓	No	✗	✗	No	?	✗	labor disputes
Krey	UB	✓	✓	✓	No	✓	✗	No	?	✓	labor disputes
Louis Rich	MO	✗	✓	✓	No	✓	✓	Yes	✗	?	cigarettes
New Traditions	HRL	✓	✓	✗	No	✓	✗	No	✓	✗	labor disputes

Company or Product	Abbr.	$	♀	⚖	(No)	🐾	⚒	⚛	🕊	💀	ALERT
Old Smokehouse	HRL	✔	✓	✗	No	✓	✗	No	✓	✗	labor disputes
Originals	TYSN	?	✓	✗	No	✓	✗	No	✓	✗	
Oscar Mayer	MO	✗	✓	✓	No	?	✓	Yes	✗	?	cigarettes
Partridge	UB	✓	✓	✓	No	✓	✗	No	?	✓	labor disputes
Peyton	UB	✓	✓	✓	No	✓	✗	No	?	✓	labor disputes
Quick Cuts	TYSN	?	✓	✗	No	✓	✗	No	✓	✗	
Rath Black Hawk	UB	✓	✓	✓	No	✓	✗	No	?	✓	labor disputes
Rodeo	UB	✓	✓	✓	No	✓	✗	No	?	✓	labor disputes
Sandwich Mate	BN	✗	✓	✓	No	✓	✓	Yes●	✓	✓	
Scott Petersen	UB	✓	✓	✓	No	✓	✗	No	?	✓	labor disputes

✔ = Top Rating   ✓ = Middle Rating   ✗ = Bottom Rating   ? = Insufficient Information
For a more detailed explanation see key on page 10

REFRIGERATED MEATS

REFRIGERATED MEATS

Company or Product	Abbr.	$	⚥	🕊	🦅	✊	🐇	⚛	🌐	🐾	ALERT
Shorgood	CAG	?	✓	No	?	✗	✓	?	?	?	OSHA fines
Soylami#	TFC	✗	✓	No	✓	✓	?	No	✓	✓	
Surrey Farm	BTC	✓+	✓	No	?	?	?	No	?	✓	
Table Trim	UB	✓	✓	No	✓	✓	✗	No	?	✓	labor disputes
Tobin's First prize	UB	✓	✓	No	✓	✓	✗	No	?	✓	labor disputes
Tom Sawyer	UB	✓	✓	No	✓	✓	✗	No	?	✓	labor disputes
Tyson	TYSN	?	✓	No	✗	✓	✗	No	?	✗	
Weaver	HFF	✗	✗	No	?	✗	?	No	✗	?	
White Rose	DIG	?	✓	No	?	?	?	No	✓	✗	
Wilson Masterpiece	WF	?	?	No	?	?	?	No	?	✗	
SALAD DRESSINGS AND MAYONNAISE											
21st Century Foods#	TFC	✗	✓	No	✓	✓	?	No	?	✓	

Company or Product	Abbr.	⚥	#	✈	✋	🐾	☢	🤝	🌍	ALERT
Bama	BN	✗	✔	No	✔	✔	✔	No	Yes●	✔	
Bernstein's	CBI	✔+	✔	No	?	✔	✔	No	?	?	
Best Foods	CPC	✗	✔	No	?	✔	✔	No	No	✔	
Cardini#	DFAM	?	✔	No	✔	✔	✔	No	No	✔	
Cardini's#	DFAM	?	✔	No	✔	✔	✔	No	No	✔	
Catalina	MO	✗	✔	No	✔	✔	✔	Yes	?	?	cigarettes
Chirat	CPC	✗	✔	No	✔	✔	✔	No	✔	✔	
Classic Herb	MO	✗	✔	No	?	✔	✔	Yes	✗	?	cigarettes
Conzelo	MO	✗	✔	No	?	✔	✔	Yes	✗	?	cigarettes
Eggo	K	✔	✔	No	?	✔	✔	No	Yes●	✔	

✔ = Top Rating   ✓ = Middle Rating   ✗ = Bottom Rating   ? = Insufficient Information

For a more detailed explanation see key on page 10

SALAD DRESSINGS AND MAYONNAISE

SALAD DRESSINGS AND MAYONNAISE

Company or Product	Abbr.	💲	⚥	✈	[icon]	⚛	[icon]	[icon]	[icon]	ALERT
El Molino#	AMH	?	✓	No	✓	No	✓	?	✗	
General Foods	MO	✗	✓	No	✓	Yes	✓	✗	?	cigarettes
Good Seasons	MO	✗	✓	No	✓	Yes	✓	✗	?	cigarettes
Hellman's	CPC	✓	✓	No	✓	No	✓	✓	✓	
Hidden Valley Ranch	CLX	✓	✓	No	✓*	No	✓	✓	✓	
Hoffman House	DF	?	?	No	✓	No	✓	?	✗	
Kraft	MO	✗	✓	No	✓*	Yes	✓	✗	?	cigarettes
Lipton	UN	✗	✓	No	?	Yes†	✓	✓	?	
Marie's	CPB	✓	✓	No	?	No	✓	✓	✓	on-site daycare
Mayacamas#	MAYA	?	?	No	?	No	✗	?	✗	
Miracle Whip	MO	✗	✓	No	✓	Yes	✗	✗	?	cigarettes
Mrs. Weavers	DF	?	✓	No	?	No	✗	?	✗	

Company or Product	Abbr.	$	⚥	✊	✈	🐰	👥	⚛	🌿	👪	ALERT
Nalley's Fine Foods	CBI	✓+	✓	?	No	?	✓	No	?	✓	
Natura#	NFS	?	?	?	No	✓	✗	No	✓	?	
Newman's Own	NEWO	✓+	✓	✗	No	✓	✓	No	✓	✓	profit to charity
Puritan	PG	✓	✓	✓	No	✓(*)	✓	Yes	✓	✓	disposable diapers
Seven Seas	MO	✗	✓	✓	No	?	✓	Yes	✗	?	cigarettes
The Source	DFAM	?	✓	✓	No	✓	✓	No	✓	✓	
Thousand Island	MO	✗	✓	✓	No	?	✓	Yes	✗	?	cigarettes
Vegetarian Pate#	TFC	✗	✓	✓	No	✓	?	No	✓	✓	
Viva	MO	✗	✓	✓	No	?	✓	Yes	✗	?	cigarettes
Weight Watchers	HNZ	✓	✓	✗	No	✓	✓	Yes	✓	✓	dolphins caught

✓ = Top Rating   ◑ = Middle Rating   ✗ = Bottom Rating   ? = Insufficient Information
For a more detailed explanation see key on page 10

SALAD DRESSINGS AND MAYONNAISE

SALT, SEASONING AND SPICES

Company or Product	Abbr.	$	♀	🐾	✈	🤝	⚛	🌐	?	ALERT
Wishbone	UN	✗	✓	No	✓*	✓	No	Yes†	?	
Accent	WH	✓	✓	No	✓○	✗	No	No	?	
ADOBO	UN	✗	✓	No	✓*	✗	No	Yes†	?	
Bac-O-Bits	GIS	✓+	✓	No	✓	✓	No	No	✓	
Basic Herbs#	AMH	?	✓	No	✓	✗	No	No	✗	
El Molino	BN	✗	✓	No	✓	✓	No	Yes●	✓	
Emperor's Kitchen	GES	?	✓	No	✓	✗	No	No	✗	
Evon's#	JSAN	?	✗	No	✓	?	No	No	✓	
Health Valley Nat. Foods#	HVAL	?	✓	No	?	?	No	No	✗	
Knorr	CPC	✗	✓	No	✓	✓	No	No	✓	
Lawry's	UN	✗	✓	No	✓*	✓	No	Yes†	?	

SALT, SEASONING AND SPICES

Company or Product	Abbr.	💲	⚥	✈	🔧	🐾	⚛	👥	🌿	ALERT
Little Pancho	BN	✗	✓	No	✓	✓	Yes●	✓	✓	
McCormick	MCRK	✓+	✓	No	?	✓	No	✓	✗	
Modern Products#	MOD	?	✓	No	?	✓	No	?	?	
Molly McButter	ACV	?	✓	No	✗	✓	No	?	?	
Roger's Foods	UFC	✓	✓	No	✓	✓	No	✓	?	
Season-All	MCRK	✓+	✓	No	?	✓	No	✓	✗	
Spice Garden#	MOD	?	✓	No	✓	✓	No	?	?	
Spike Brand#	MOD	?	?	No	✓	✓	No	?	?	
Vegetable Supreme	MCRK	✓+	✓	No	✓	✓	No	✓	✗	

✓ = Top Rating   ✓ = Middle Rating   ✗ = Bottom Rating   ? = Insufficient Information
For a more detailed explanation see key on page 10

SHAVING NEEDS

Company or Product	Abbr.	💲	⚥	♻	✈	🐇	⚛				🌿	ALERT
Aqua-Velva	BECH	?	?	?	No	✗○	✓	?	No	Yes†	?	✓	
Atra	GS	✓	✓	✓	No	✗	✓	✓	No	Yes●	✓	✓	
Barbasol	PFE	✓	✓	✓	No	✓(●)	✓	✓	No	Yes●	✓	✗	heart-valve suit
Brut	FAB	?	?	?	No	✗	✗	?	No	No	✓	?	
Colgate	CL	✓+	✓	✓	No	✓*	✓	✓	No	Yes*	✓	✓	
Edge Gel	SCJ	✓+	✓	✓	No	✗	✓	✓	No	Yes●	✓	✓	1st to ban CFC's
Gillette	GS	✓	✓	✓	No	✗	✓	✓	No	Yes●	✓	✓	
Good News!	GS	✓	✓	✗	No	✗	✗	✓	No	Yes●	✓	✓	
Nair	CAR	?	?	?	No	✗○	✓	?	No	No	✓	?	
Neet	AHP	✗	✗	✗	No	✓(●)	✓	✓	No	Yes*	✓	✗	infant formula
Noxzema	NOXL	✓+	✓	✓	No	✓	✓	✓	No	No	✓	✗	

Company or Product	Abbr.	$	♀					⚛				ALERT
Old Spice	ACY	✔	?	No	✘○	✔	✔	No	Yes*	✘	✓	makes pesticides
Orjene Nat. Cosmetics#	ORJ	?	?	No	✔	✔	✘	No	No	✘	✘	
Paul Penders#	PP	?	✘	No	✔	✔	✘	No	No	✘	✔	
Personal Touch	WLA	✔	✓	No	✘○	✔	✔	No	Yes●	✔	✔	
Schick	WLA	✔	✓	No	✘○	✔	✔	No	Yes●	✔	✓	
Tom's of Maine#	TOM	✔+	✘	No	✔	✔	✔	No	No	✔	✓	
Trac II	GS	✔	✓	No	✔	✔	✔	No	Yes●	✔	✔	
Ultrasmooth	BMY	✔	✔	No	✔(*)	✓○	✔	No	Yes*	?	✘	infant formula
Williams Lectric Shave	BECH	?	?	No	✘○	?	?	No	Yes†	?	✔	

✔ = Top Rating   ✓ = Middle Rating   ✘ = Bottom Rating   ? = Insufficient Information

For a more detailed explanation see key on page 10

SHAVING NEEDS

SHORTENINGS AND OIL

Company or Product	Abbr.	$	O+	⚖	✈	⚛	🐇	ALERT
SHORTENINGS AND OIL								
Archer's	ADM	?	✓	?	No	?	No	✗	
Arrowhead Mills #	AM	?	✓	?	No	?	No	✓	
Bake-Rite	WF	?	?	?	No	?	No	✗	
Crisco	PG	✓	✓	✓	No	(✓*)	Yes	✓	disposable diapers
E-Z Chef	MO	✗	✓+	✓	No	✓	Yes	?	cigarettes
Hunt's	BTC	✓+	✓	?	No	?	No	✓	
Loriva #	LOR	?	?	✓	No	✓	No	?	
Mazola	CPC	✗	✓	✓	No	✓	No	✓	
Old Monk #	DFAM	?	?	✓	No	✓	No	✓	
Orville Redenbacher's	BTC	✓+	✓	?	No	?	No	✓	
Planters	RJR	✓	✓	✓	No	?	Yes*	✗	cigarettes

Company or Product	Abbr.	$										ALERT
Progresso	WH	✓	✓	?	✓	No	✓○	✗	No	?	✓	
Protein-Aide#	LOR	?	?	?	✓	No	✓	✗	No	?	✓	
Puritan	PG	✓	✓	✓	✓	No	✓(*)	✓	Yes	✓	✓	disposable diapers
Purlite	CPC	✗	✓	✓	✓	No	✓	✓	No	✓	✓	
Sunlite	BTC	✓+	✓	✓	✓	No	?	?	No	✓	✓	
Wesson	BTC	✓+	✓	✓	✓	No	?	?	No	✓	✓	
SKIN CARE AIDS												
Anbesol	AHP	✗	✓	✗	✓	No	✓(*)	✓	No	✓	✗	infant formula
Aubrey Organics#	AUB	?	✓	✓	✓	No	✓	✓	No	✓	✓	
Aura Cacia#	AURA	?	✓	✓	✓	No	✓	✓	No	✓	✓	

✓ = Top Rating ✓ = Middle Rating ✗ = Bottom Rating ? = Insufficient Information

For a more detailed explanation see key on page 10

Page 197

SKIN CARE AIDS

Company or Product	Abbr.	💲	♀	☢	✈	🐰	🔬	⚛	🌸	🍃	ALERT
Autumn Harp#	AUT	?	✓	✗	No	✓	✓	No	✓	✓	
Avon	AVP	✓	✓	✓	No	✓	✓	No	✓	✓	
Biotene H24	CARM	?	✓	✓	No	✓	?	Yes	✓	✓	
Calgon	BECH	?	?	✓	No	✗○	?	Yes†	?	✓	
Carme	CARM	?	✓	✓	No	✓	?	Yes	✓	✓	
Chesebrough–Ponds	UN	✗	✓	✓	No	✓*	✗	Yes†	?	?	infant formula
Clairol	BMY	✓	✓	✓	No	✓(*)	✓	Yes*	?	✗	
Clearasil	PG	✓	✓	✓	No	✓(*)	✓	Yes	✓	✓	disposable diapers
Coppertone	SGP	✓	✓	✓	No	✓(*)	?	Yes●	✓	✓	
Country Roads	CARM	?	✓	✓	No	✓	✓	Yes	✓	✓	
Curel	SCJ	✓+	✓	✓	No	✓	✓	Yes●	✓	✓	1st. to ban CFC's
Desitin	PFE	✓	✓	✓	No	✓(*)	✓	Yes●	✓	✗	heart-valve suit

Company or Product	Abbr.	💲	⚥	◻	◻	◻	◻	◻	◻	◻	ALERT
Elastin	CARM	?	✓	No	✓	?	No	✓	?	✓	
Faberge	FAB	?	?	No	✗	?	No	✗	?	✓	
Jojoba Farms	CARM	?	✓	No	✓	?	Yes	✓	?	✓	
Lip Sense#	AUT	?	✓	No	✗	?	No	✗	?	✓	
Lip Trip#	MOUN	?	✓	No	✗	✗	No	✓	✗	✗	
Lubriderm	WLA	✓	✓	No	✗○	✓	Yes●	✓	✓	✓	
Mill Creek	CARM	?	✓	No	✓	?	Yes	✓	?	✓	
Moisture Formula	JPC	?	✓	No	✓	?	No	✗	?	✗	
Mountain Ocean#	MOUN	?	✓	No	✗	✗	No	✓	✗	✗	
Natural Lips#	AUB	?	✓	No	✓	✓	No	✓	✓	✓	

✓ = Top Rating   ✓ = Middle Rating   ✗ = Bottom Rating   ? = Insufficient Information

For a more detailed explanation see key on page 10

SKIN CARE AIDS

SKIN CARE AIDS

Company or Product	Abbr.	💲	♀				⚛			ALERT
Nature's Herbs#	HERB	?	✗	?	No	✓	?	No	No	?	
Noxema	NOXL	✓+	✗	✓	No	✓	✓	No	No	✗	
Oil of Olay	PG	✓	✓	No	✓(*)	✓	No	No	Yes	✓	disposable diapers
Orjene Nat. Cosmetics#	ORJ	?	?	No	✓	✓	No	No	No	✗	
Paul Penders#	PP	?	✗	No	✓	✓	No	No	No	✓	
Phisoderm	EK	✓	✓	Yes	✓(*)	✓	No	No	No	✓	
Pond's	UN	✗	✓	No	✓*	✓	No	No	Yes†	?	
Rachel Perry#	RP	✗	?	No	✓	✓	No	No	No	✓	
Reviva Labs#	REV	?	?	No	✓	✓	No	No	No	✓	
Richardson-Vicks	PG	✓	✓	No	✓(*)	✓	No	No	Yes	✓	disposable diapers
Rosa Mosqueta#	AUB	?	✓	No	✓	✓	No	No	No	✓	
Schiff	IBC	?	✗	No	✓	?	No	No	No	✗	

Company or Product	Abbr.	$	♀	[icon]	[icon]	✈	[icon]	[hands]	⚛	[animal]	ALERT
Sea Breeze	BMY	✔	✔	✔	✔	No	✔	✔	No	Yes*	?	infant formula
Skin Trip#	MOUN	?	✔	✗	✔	No	✔(*)	✗	No	No	✔	
Soft Sense	SCJ	✔+	✔	✔	✔	No	✗	✔	No	Yes●	✔	1st to ban CFC's
Solgar Company	SLGR	?	?	?	?	No	?	?	No	?	?	
Stridex	EK	✔	✔	✔	✔	Yes	✔(*)	✔	No	No	✔	
Twin Labs	TWIN	?	✔	✔	✔	No	✔	?	No	No	✔	
Ultra Care#	AUT	?	✗	✔	✔	No	✗	?	No	No	✔	
Ultra Sheen	JPC	?	✔	✔	✔	No	✔	?	No	No	✗	
Vaseline	UN	✗	✔	✔	✔	No	✔*	✗	No	Yes†	?	
Wondra	PG	✔	✔	✔	✔	No	✔(*)	✔	No	Yes	✔	disposable diapers

✔ = Top Rating ✓ = Middle Rating ✗ = Bottom Rating ? = Insufficient Information
For a more detailed explanation see key on page 10

SKIN CARE AIDS

SNACKS

Company or Product	Abbr.	💲	♀	✊	✈	☯	⚛	🌍	ALERT
SNACKS									
21st Century Foods#	TFC	✗	✓	✓	No	✓	?	No	✓	
Almost Home	RJR	✓	✓	✓	No	?	✓	No	Yes*	✗	cigarettes
Andy Capp	GIS	✓+	✓	✓	No	✓	✓	No	No	✓	
Arrowhead Mills#	AM	?	✓	✓	No	✓	?	No	No	✓	
Barbara's Bakery#	BARB	?	✓	✓	No	✓	✓	No	No	✗	
Barnum's Animals	RJR	✓	✓	✓	No	?	✓	No	Yes*	✗	cigarettes
Barrel O' Fun	BN	✗	✓	✓	No	✓	✓	No	Yes●	✓	
BeeBo	FLO	?	✓	?	No	✓	?	No	No	✗	
Betsy's#	BARB	?	✓	✓	No	✓	✓	No	No	✓	
Betty Crocker	GIS	✓+	✓	✓	No	✓	✓	No	No	✓	
Blue Bird	FLO	?	✗	?	No	?	✓	No	No	✗	

Company or Product	Abbr.	$	♀	✈	[icon]	[icon]	⚛	[icon]	ALERT
Borden	BN	✗	✓	No	✓	✓	No	✓	
Br. Ron Products	KFS	?	✓	No	✓	✗	No	✓	
Bravos	BN	✗	✓	No	✓	✓	Yes●	✓	
Buck Eye	BN	✗	✓	No	✓	✓	Yes●	✓	
Bugles	GIS	✓+	✓	No	✓	✓	No	✓	
Cain's	BN	✗	✓	No	✓	✓	Yes●	✓	
Cape Cod	BUD	✓+	✓	No	✓	✓	No	✓	
Chee-tos	PEP	✓	✓	No	?	✓	Yes	✓	
Cheez Doodles	BN	✗	✓	No	✓	✓	Yes●	✓	
Cheez Links	MO	✗	✓	No	?	✓	Yes	✗	cigarettes

✓ = Top Rating ✓ = Middle Rating ✗ = Bottom Rating ? = Insufficient Information
For a more detailed explanation see key on page 10

SNACKS

Company or Product	Abbr.	$	♀	[icon]	✈	[icon]	[icon]	⚛	[globe]	[icon]	ALERT
Cheez Whiz	MO	✗	✓	No	?	✓	No	Yes	✗	?	cigarettes
Chesty	BN	✗	✓	No	✓	✓	No	Yes●	✓	✓	
Chex	RAL	✗	✗	No	✓	✓	No	No	✓	✗	dolphins caught
Chip-A-Roos	RJR	✓	✓	No	✓	✓	No	Yes*	✗	✗	cigarettes
Chips Ahoy	RJR	✓	✓	No	?	✓	No	Yes*	✗	✗	cigarettes
Christie	RJR	✓	✓	No	?	✓	No	Yes*	✗	✗	cigarettes
Clover Ridge	MO	✗	✓	No	?	✗	No	Yes	✗	?	cigarettes
Combos	MARS	?	?	No	?	✓	No	No	?	?	
Corn Diggers	RJR	✓	✓	No	?	✓	No	Yes*	✗	?	cigarettes
Cornies	BN	✗	✓	No	✓	✓	No	Yes●	✓	✓	
Cottage Fries	BN	✗	✓	No	✓	✓	No	Yes●	✓	✓	
Cracker Jack	BN	✗	✓	No	✓	✓	No	Yes●	✓	✓	

Company or Product	Abbr.	💲	👤	🌐	⚛	🐾			Yes/No			ALERT
Crane	BN	✗	✗	✓	✔	No	✔	✔	✓	No	Yes●	✓	
Crunch 'n Munch	AHP	✗	✗	✓	✔⊛	No	✓	✔	✗	No	Yes*	✗	infant formula
Dean	DF	?	✓	✓	?	No	✗	✓	?	No	No	✗	
Deer Valley Farm #	DVF	✗	✓	✓	✔	No	?	✔	✓	No	No	✗	
Del Monte	RJR	✔	✔	✓	✔	No	?	✓	✔	No	Yes*	✗	cigarettes
Delta Gold	PEP	✓	✓	✓	✓	No	✔	✓	✓	No	Yes	✓	
Deluxe Grahams	UBH	?	?	✓	?	No	?	✓	?	No	No	✗	
Dipsy Doodles	BN	✗	✔	✔	✔	No	✓	✔	✓	No	Yes●	✓	
Dole	CKE	?	?	✗	?	No	✗	✗	✗	No	No	✗	pesticide use
Doritos	PEP	✔	✔	✓	✔	No	✔	✓	✓	No	Yes	✓	

✔ = Top Rating   ✓ = Middle Rating   ✗ = Bottom Rating   ? = Insufficient Information

For a more detailed explanation see key on page 10

SNACKS

Company or Product	Abbr.	💲	♀	⛰	🌲	✎	⚗⊛	⚛	🌐	🐾	ALERT
Duncan Hines	PG	✓	✓	✓	No	✓	✓⊛	No	Yes	✓	disposable diapers
E.L. Fudge	UBH	?	?	?	No	✓	?	No	No	✗	
Eagle Snacks	BUD	✓+	✓	✗	No	✓	✓	No	No	✓	
Eden#	EDEN	✗	✗	✓	No	✓	✓	No	No	✗	
El Dorado	BN	✗	✓	✓	No	✓	✓	Yes●	No	✓	
El Molino#	AMH	?	?	?	No	✗	✗	No	No	✗	
El Molino	BN	✗	✓	✓	No	✓	✓	Yes●	No	✓	
Evangeline Maid	FLO	?	✗	?	No	✓	✓	No	No	✗	
Evon's#	JSAN	?	✓	✗	No	✓	?	No	No	✓	
Falcon Trading#	FALC	?	✓	✗	No	✓	✓	No	No	✗	
Fig Newtons	RJR	✓	?	?	No	✓	?	Yes*	No	✗	cigarettes
Frito-Lay	PEP	✓	✓	✓	No	✓	✓	Yes	Yes	✓	

Company or Product	Abbr.	💲	◻	◻	◻	◻	◻	◻	◻	◻	ALERT
Fritos	PEP	✓	✓	✓	No	✓	✓	No	√	✓	
Fruit Wrinkles	GIS	✓+	✓+	✓	No	✓	✓	No	√	✓	
Fruit Roll-Ups	GIS	✓+	✓+	√	No	✓	✓	No	√	✓	
Fruit Slush	UN	✗	✗	✓	No	√*	✓	Yes†	?	?	
Fruit Corners	GIS	✓+	✓+	✓	No	✓	✓	No	√	✓	
Fudge Stripes	UBH	?	?	√	No	?	√	No	?	√	
FunYuns	PEP	✓	✓	✓	No	✓	✓	No	✓	√	
Garden of Eatin'*#	GEAT	?	?	√	No	√	√	No	√	✓	
Geiser's	BN	✗	✗	√	No	√	√	Yes●	√	√	
Giggles	RJR	✓	√	√	No	?	√	Yes*	✗	✗	cigarettes

✓ = Top Rating   √ = Middle Rating   ✗ = Bottom Rating   ? = Insufficient Information

For a more detailed explanation see key on page 10

SNACKS

Company or Product	Abbr.	💲	♀	👤	✈	🐾	🧑	⚛	👪	🌐	🐢	ALERT
Grandma's	PEP	✓	✓	?	No	✓	✓	No	Yes	✓	✓	
Granola Dipps	OAT	✓	✓	✓	No	✓	✓	No	No	✓	✓	
Guy's	BN	✗	✓	✓	No	✓	✓	No	Yes●	✓	✓	cigarettes
Handi-Snacks	MO	✗	✓	?	No	✓	✓	No	Yes	✗	?	
Hawaiian Kettle	BUD	✓+	✓	✓	No	✓	?	No	No	✓	✓	
Health Valley Nat. Foods#	HVAL	?	✓	?	No	✓	?	No	No	?	?	
Honey Maid	RJR	✓	✓	?	No	✓	✓	No	Yes*	✗	✗	cigarettes
Hostess	RAL	✗	✓	✗	No	✓	✓	No	No	✗	✗	dolphins caught
Hydrox	AMB	✗	✓	✗	No	✓	?	No	Yes	?	✗	cigarettes
Indian Brand	BN	✗	✓	✓	No	✓	✓	No	Yes●	✓	✓	
Jays	BN	✗	✓	✓	No	✓	✓	No	Yes●	✓	✓	
Jiffy Pop	AHP	✗	✓	✗	No	✓(⊛)	✓	No	Yes*	✓	✗	infant formula

Company or Product	Abbr.	💲#	⚥	✈	🤝	✊	⚛	🐇	🐝	ALERT
KAS	BN	✗	✔	No	✔	✔	No	Yes	✔	
Keebler	UBH	?	?	No	✔	?	No	No	✗	
Kellogg's	K	✔	✔	No	✔	✔	No	Yes	✔	
Kiddy Clover	BN	✗	✔	No	✔	✔	No	Yes	✔	
Krunchers!	BN	✗	✔	No	✗	✔	No	Yes	✔	
Kudos	MARS	?	?	No	✔	?	No	No	?	
La Famous	BN	✗	✔	No	✔	✔	No	Yes	✔	
Laura Scudder's	BN	✗	✔	No	✔	✔	No	Yes	✔	
Lay's	PEP	✔	✔	No	✔	✔	No	Yes	✔	
Lifetone International#	LFTI	?	✗	No	✗	✔	No	No	?	

✔ = Top Rating   ✓ = Middle Rating   ✗ = Bottom Rating   ? = Insufficient Information
For a more detailed explanation see key on page 10

SNACKS

Company or Product	Abbr.	$	♀	[icon]	[✈]	[icon]	[⚛]	[icon]	[icon]	ALERT
Little Pancho	BN	✗	✓	✓	No	✓	Yes●	✓	✓	
Lorna Doone	RJR	✓	✓	✓	No	?	Yes*	✗	✗	cigarettes
Mallomars	RJR	✓	✓	✓	No	?	Yes*	✗	✗	cigarettes
Mister Salty	RJR	✓	✓	✓	No	?	Yes*	✗	✗	cigarettes
Mohawk	MO	✗	✓	✓	No	?	Yes	✓	?	cigarettes
Munchos	PEP	✓	✓	✓	No	✓	Yes	✗	✓	
Nabisco	RJR	✓	✓	✓	No	?	Yes*	✗	✗	cigarettes
Nalley's	CBI	✓+	?	?	No	✓	No	?	✓	
Natura#	NFS	?	?	?	No	✗	No	✓	?	
Nature's Own	FLO	?	?	?	No	?	No	?	✗	
New Mill	BN	✗	✓	✓	No	✓	Yes●	✓	✓	
New York Deli	BN	✗	✓	✓	No	✓	Yes●	✓	✓	

Company or Product	Abbr.	💲	⚥	🗻✈		🔬	⚛			ALERT
Newman's Own	NEWO	✓+	✓	✗	No	✓	✓	No	✓	✓	profit to charity
Newtons	RJR	✓	✓	✓	No	?	✓	Yes*	✗	✗	cigarettes
Nilla	RJR	✓	✓	✓	No	?	✓	Yes*	✗	✗	cigarettes
Nutter Butter	RJR	✓	✓	✓	No	?	✓	Yes*	✗	✗	cigarettes
O-Ke-Doke	BN	✗	✓	✓	No	✓	✓	No·	✓	✓	
O'Grady's	PEP	✓	✓	✓	No	?	✓	Yes	✓	✓	
Oreos	RJR	✓	✓	✓	No	?	✓	Yes*	✓	✗	cigarettes
Orville Redenbacher's	BTC	✓+	✓	?	No	?	✓	No	✓	✓	
Pacific Gardens#	ACOP	?	✗	✗	No	✓	✓	No	✓	✓	
Pepitos	BN	✗	✓	✓	No	✓	✓	Yes●	✓	✓	

✓ = Top Rating   ✓ = Middle Rating   ✗ = Bottom Rating   ? = Insufficient Information

For a more detailed explanation see key on page 10

SNACKS

Company or Product	Abbr.	$	♀					⚛			ALERT
Pepperidge Farm	CPB	✓	✓	✓	No	✓	✓	No	✓	✓	on-site daycare
Pick Ups	BN	✗	?	✓	No	?	✓	Yes●	✓	✓	
Pillsbury	GMP	?	?	?	?	✓	?	Yes†	?	?	dolphins Caught
Planters	RJR	✓	✓	✓	No	?	✓	Yes*	✓	✗	cigarettes
Pop Tarts	K	✓	✓	✓	No	✓	✓	Yes●	✓	✓	
Pop Secret	GIS	✓+	✓	✓	No	✓	✓	No	✓	✓	
Pringles	PG	✓	✓	✓	No	✓(*)	✓	Yes	✓	✓	disposable diapers
Quaker	OAT	✗	✓	✗	No	✓	✓	No	✓	✗	
Ralston	RAL	✗	✓	✓	No	✓	✓	No	✓	✓	dolphins caught
Red Seal	BN	✗	✓	✓	No	✓	✓	Yes●	✓	✓	
Ridgies	BN	✗	✓	✓	No	✓	✓	Yes●	✓	✓	
Ritz	RJR	✓	✓	✓	No	?	?	Yes*	✗	✗	cigarettes

Company or Product	Abbr.	⚥$	♀	✈	🗺	🏃	🐾	☢	📋	♻	ALERT
Rold Gold	PEP	✔	✔	No	✔	?	✔	No	Yes	✓	
Ruffles	PEP	✔	✔	No	✔	?	✔	No	Yes	✓	
Salsa Rio	PEP	✔	✔	No	✔	?	✔	No	Yes	✓	
Seyferts	BN	✗	✓	No	✔	✓	✓	No	Yes●	✓	
Shreddies	RJR	✔	✗	No	✔	✔	?	No	Yes*	✗	cigarettes
Snack Time	BN	✗	✔	No	✓	✔	✓	No	Yes●	✓	
Snyder	CBI	✔+	✓	No	?	✔	✓	No	No	?	
Soft Batch	UBH	?	?	No	?	✓	?	No	No	?	
Spirals	BN	✗	✓	No	✔	✔	✓	No	Yes●	✗	
Sunkist	UN	✗	✓	No	✓	✔	✗	No	Yes†	?	

✔ = Top Rating ✓ = Middle Rating ✗ = Bottom Rating ? = Insufficient Information

For a more detailed explanation see key on page 10

SNACKS

SNACKS

Company or Product	Abbr.	💲	♀	✈	(icon)	(icon)	⚛	(icon)	(icon)	ALERT
Sweet Cloud Munchies#	GES	?	✓	No	✓	✗	No	No	✓	✗
TastyKake	TBC	✓+	✓	No	✓	✓	No	No	✓	✓
Teddy Grahams	RJR	✓	✗	No	✓	?	No	Yes*	✗	✗	cigarettes
Toll House	NEST	?	?	No	?	✗	No	Yes†	?	✗	infant formula
Tor-Ticos	BN	✗	✓	No	✓	✓	No	Yes●	✓	✓
Tostitos	PEP	✓	?	No	✓	✓	No	Yes	✓	✓
Vegetarian Health#	VH	?	?	No	✓	?	No	No	?	?
Vegetarian Pate#	TFC	✗	✓	No	✓	?	No	No	✓	✓
Walker's Crisps	RJR	✓	✓	No	✓	?	No	Yes*	✗	✗	cigarettes
Whipps	OAT	✓	✓	No	✓	✓	No	No	✓	✓
White Cloud	PG	✓	✓	No	✓(*)	✓	No	Yes	✓	✓	disposable diapers
Wise	BN	✗	✓	No	✓	✗	No	Yes●	✓	✓

Company or Product	Abbr.	💲	♀⊕			✈		⚛		🕊	ALERT
Wyler's	UN	✘	✓	No	✓	✓	✘	No	Yes†	?	
Yum-Yums	AMB	✓	✘	No	✓	?	?	No	Yes	✓	cigarettes
SOAPS — HAND & BATH											
Aroma Vera*	AV	?	✓	No	✓	✓	?	No	No	✘	
Aubrey Organics#	AUB	?	✓	No	✓	✓	✓	No	No	✓	
Aura Cacia#	AURA	?	✓	No	✓	✓	✓	No	No	✓	
Avon	AVP	✓	✓	No	✓	✓	✓	No	No	✓	
Boraxo	G	?	✓	No	✓	✓	✓	No	No	?	
Calgon	BECH	?	?	No	✓	✘○	?	No	Yes†	?	
Camay	PG	✓	✓	No	✓	✓(*)	✓	No	Yes	✓	disposable diapers

✓ = Top Rating   ✓ = Middle Rating   ✘ = Bottom Rating   ? = Insufficient Information
For a more detailed explanation see key on page 10

SOAPS - HAND & BATH

SOAPS - HAND & BATH

Company or Product	Abbr.	$	♀+	(icon)	✈	(icon)	(icon)	(icon)	⚛	(icon)	(icon)	ALERT
Caress	UN	✗	✓	✓	No	✓*	✓	✗	No	Yes†	?	?	
Caribee	UN	✗	✓	✓	No	✓*	✓	✗	No	Yes†	?	?	
Carme	CARM	?	✓	✓	No	✓*	✓	?	No	Yes	✓	✓	
Cashmere Bouquet	CL	✓+	✓	✓	No	✓(*)	✓	✓	No	Yes*	✓	✓	
Clear Complexion	AMB	✓	✗	✗	No	✓	✓	?	No	Yes	?	✓	cigarettes
Coast	PG	✓	✓	✓	No	✓	✓	✓	No	Yes	✓	✓	disposable diapers
Country Roads	CARM	?	✓	✓	No	✓	✓	?	No	Yes	✓	✓	
Dial	G	?	✓	✓	No	✓*	✓	✓	No	No	?	✓	
Dove	UN	✗	✗	✓	No	✓(*)	✓	✗	No	Yes†	?	?	
Dreft	PG	✓	✓	✓	No	✓*	✓	✓	No	Yes	✓	✓	disposable diapers
Irish Spring	CL	✓+	✓	✓	No	✓*	✓	✓	No	Yes*	✓	✓	
Ivory	PG	✓	✓	✓	No	✓(*)	✓	✓	No	Yes	✓	✓	disposable diapers

Company or Product	Abbr.	💲	♀	◻	✈	🐇	◻	◻	⚛	◻	👪	ALERT
Johnson & Johnson	JNJ	√	✓	✓	No	✓(*)	✓	✓	No	Yes*	✓	✓	
Loanda	CARM	?	✓	√	No	✓	✓	?	No	Yes	√	√	
Lux	UN	✗	✓	√	No	✓*	✓	✗	No	Yes†	?	?	
Milk Creek	CARM	?	√	√	No	✓*	✓	?	No	Yes	√	√	
Neutro Balance	CL	✓+	✓	√	No	✓*	✓	√	No	Yes*	✓	✓	
Orjene Nat. Cosmetics#	ORJ	?	?	✓	No	✓	✓	✗	No	No	√	✗	
Palmolive	CL	✓+	✓	√	No	✓*	✓	√	No	Yes*	√	✓	
Paul Penders#	PP	?	√	√	No	✓	✓	✗	No	No	✓	✓	
Pure & Natural	G	?	√	✓	No	✓	✓	√	No	No	√	?	
Reviva Labs#	REV	?	✓	√	No	✓	✓	✗	No	No	√	✗	

✓ = Top Rating √ = Middle Rating ✗ = Bottom Rating ? = Insufficient Information

For a more detailed explanation see key on page 10

SOAPS - HAND & BATH

Company or Product	Abbr.	$	⚥	[icon]	[icon]	[icon]	[icon]	[atom]	[icon]	[icon]	ALERT
Rosa Mosqueta#	AUB	?	✓	✓	No	✓	✓	No	✓	✓	
Safeguard	PG	✓	✓	✓	No	✓(*)	✓	Yes	✓	✓	disposable diapers
Sandcastle Aromatherapy#	AURA	?	✓	✓	No	✓	✓	No	✓	✓	
Schiff	IBC	?	✓	✗	No	✓	?	No	?	✗	
Shield	UN	✗	✓	✓	No	✓*	✗	Yes†	✓	?	
Solgar Company	SLGR	?	?	?	No	?	?	No	?	?	
Tom's of Maine#	TOM	✓+	✓	✗	No	✓	✓	No	✓	✓	
Tone	G	?	✓	✓	No	✓	✓	No	✓	?	
Zest	PG	✓	✓	✓	No	✓(*)	✓	Yes	✓	✓	disposable diapers
SOAPS & DETERGENT											
Ajax	CL	✓+	✓	✓	No	✓*	✓	No	Yes*	✓	
All	UN	✗	✓	✓	No	✓*	✗	No	Yes†	?	

Company or Product	Abbr.	$	⚥	✈	🤝	🐾	⚛	🕊	ALERT
Borax	G	?	✓	No	✓	✓	No	?	
Brillo	G	?	✓	No	✓	✓	No	?	
Cascade	PG	✓	✓	No	✓(*)	✓	Yes	✓	disposable diapers
Crystal White Octagon	CL	✓+	✓	No	✓*	✓	Yes*	✓	
Dawn	PG	✓	✓	No	✓(*)	✓	Yes	✓	disposable diapers
Dermassage	CL	✓+	✓	No	✓*	✓	Yes*	✓	
Galaxy	CL	✓+	✓	No	✓*	✓	Yes*	✓	
Ivory	PG	✓	✓	No	✓(*)	✓	Yes	✓	disposable diapers
Joy	PG	✓	✓	No	✓(*)	✓	Yes	✓	disposable diapers
Lux	UN	✗	✓	No	✓*	✗	Yes†	?	

✓ = Top Rating ✓ = Middle Rating ✗ = Bottom Rating ? = Insufficient Information

For a more detailed explanation see key on page 10

SOAPS & DETERGENT

SOFT DRINKS & BEVERAGE MIXES

Company or Product	Abbr.	💲	⚥	✿	✈	✍	⚛	🐾	👥	🏠	ALERT
Palm	CL	✓+	✓	✓	No	✓*	✓	✓	No	Yes*	✓	
Palmolive	CL	✓+	✓	✓	No	✓*	✓	✓	No	Yes*	✓	
Purex Heavy-Duty	G	?	✓	✓	No	?	✓	✓	No	No	?	
Sun Light	UN	✗	✓	✓	No	✓*	✗	✓	No	Yes†	?	

SOFT DRINKS & BEVERAGE MIXES

Company or Product	Abbr.	💲	⚥	✿	✈	✍	⚛	🐾	👥	🏠	ALERT
Cactus Cooler	CADB	✓	✓	✗	No	✓	✓	✓	No	Yes†	?	
Canada Dry	CADB	✓	✓	✗	No	✓	✓	✓	No	Yes†	?	
Caribbean Cooler	MO	✗	✓	✓	No	?	✓	✓	No	Yes	?	cigarettes
Coca-Cola	KO	✓	✓	✓	No	?	✓	✓	No	Yes	✓	
Coco Lopez	BN	✗	✓	✓	No	✓	✓	✓	No	Yes●	✓	
Coke	KO	✓	✓	?	No	?	✓	✓	No	Yes	✓	
Country Foods	MO	✗	✓	✓	No	?	✓	✓	No	Yes	?	cigarettes

Company or Product	Abbr.	💲#	♀♂	✊	✈	♟	⚛	🐾	🌀	♲	ALERT
Country Time	MO	✗	✓	✓	No	?	✓	No	Yes	✗	?	cigarettes
Crystal Light	MO	✗	✓	✓	No	?	✓	No	Yes	✗	?	cigarettes
Deer Park	CLX	✓	✓	✓	No	✓*	✓	No	No	✓	✓	
Diet Sun	MO	✗	✓	✓	No	?	✓	No	Yes	✗	?	cigarettes
Edensoy#	EDEN	✗	✗	✗	No	?	✓	No	No	✓	✗	
Fanta	KO	✓	✓	✓	No	?	✓	No	Yes	✓	✓	
Five Alive	KO	✓	✓	✓	No	?	✓	No	Yes	✓	✓	
Fresca	KO	✓	✓	✓	No	?	✓	No	Yes	✓	✓	
Fruit Boxes	MO	✗	✓	✓	No	?	✓	No	Yes	✗	?	cigarettes
General Foods	MO	✗	✓	✓	No	?	✓	No	Yes	✗	?	cigarettes

✓ = Top Rating   ✓ = Middle Rating   ✗ = Bottom Rating   ? = Insufficient Information

For a more detailed explanation see key on page 10

SOFT DRINKS & BEVERAGE MIXES

SOFT DRINKS & BEVERAGE MIXES

Company or Product	Abbr.	$	♀	🌲	✊	🐾	⚛	✿	🌍	⚖	ALERT
Hawaiian Punch	RJR	✓	✓	No	?	✓	?	No	Yes*	✗	✗	cigarettes
Health Valley Nat. Foods#	HVAL	?	?	No	?	✓	?	No	No	✓	✗	
Hi-C	KO	✓	✓	No	?	✓	✓	No	Yes	✓	✓	
Ice Teasers	NEST	?	?	No	?	✓	✗	No	Yes†	?	✓	infant formula
Jake	PEP	✓	✓	No	?	✓	✓	No	Yes	✓	✓	
Kool-Aid	MO	✗	✓	No	?	✓	✓	No	Yes	✗	?	cigarettes
Le Gout	K	✓	✓	No	?	✓	✓	No	Yes●	✓	✓	
Light 'n Juicy	KO	✓	✓	No	?	✓	✓	No	Yes	✓	✓	
Lipton	UN	✗	✓	No	✓*	✓	✗	No	Yes†	?	?	
Loma Linda	LOMA	?	✓	No	?	✓	✗	No	No	✗	✗	
Mello Yello	KO	✓	✓	No	?	✓	✓	No	Yes	✓	✓	
Minute Maid	KO	✓	✓	No	?	✓	✓	No	Yes	✓	✓	

Company or Product	Abbr.	#	♀				⚛			ALERT
Mountain Dew	PEP	✓	✓	No	✓	✓	No	Yes	✓	
Mr. Pibb	KO	✓	✓	No	✓	✓	No	Yes	✓	
No-Cal	CADB	√	✗	No	✓	✓	No	Yes†	?	
Pepsi-Cola	PEP	✓	✓	No	✓	✓	No	Yes	✓	
Pepsi	PEP	✓	✓	No	✓	✓	No	Yes	✓	
Ramblin'	KO	✓	✓	No	✓	✓	No	Yes	✓	
Saratoga	MO	✗	?	No	✓	✓	No	Yes	?	cigarettes
Schweppes	CADB	√	✓	No	✗	✓	No	Yes†	✓	
Seagram's	VO	?	?	No	√	?	No	No	√	
Slice	PEP	✓	✓	No	✓	✓	No	Yes	✓	

✓ = Top Rating   √ = Middle Rating   ✗ = Bottom Rating   ? = Insufficient Information

For a more detailed explanation see key on page 10

Page 223

SOFT DRINKS & BEVERAGE MIXES

SOFT DRINKS & BEVERAGE MIXES

Company or Product	Abbr.	(#)	(♀)	(icon)	(✈)	(icon)	(Yes/No)	(icon)	(atom)	(icon)	ALERT
Sprite	KO	✓	✓	✓	No	?	✓	No	Yes	✓	✓	
Strawberry Falls	MO	✗	✓	✓	No	?	✓	No	Yes	✗	?	cigarettes
Sunkist	UN	✗	✓	✓	No	✓*	✗	No	Yes†	?	?	
Supri	MO	✓	✓	✓	No	?	✓	No	Yes	✗	?	cigarettes
Tab	KO	✗	✓	✓	No	?	✓	No	Yes	✓	✓	
Tang	MO	✓	✓	✓	No	?	✓	No	Yes	✗	?	cigarettes
TEEM	PEP	✓	✓	✓	No	?	✓	No	Yes	✓	✓	
Wyler's	UN	✗	✓	✓	No	✓*	✗	No	Yes†	?	?	
Zeltzer Seltzer	BUD	✓+	✓	✓	No	✓	✓	No	No	✓	✓	
SOUP												
Campbell's	CPB	✓	✓	✓	No	?	✓	No	No	✓	✓	on-site daycare
Chunky Soup	CPB	✓	✓	✓	No	?	✓	No	No	✓	✓	on-site daycare

Company or Product	Abbr.	💲	♀	👤	✈	⚛	🐇	(nuclear)	(info)	ALERT
Continental	UN	✖	✓	✓	No	✓*	✖	No	?	
Cup-A-Soup	UN	✖	✓	✓	No	✓*	✖	Yes†	?	
Curtice	CBI	✓+	✓	?	No	?	?	No	?	
Great American	HNZ	✓	✓	✖	No	✓	✓	Yes	✓	dolphins caught
Hain Natural	WH	✓	✓	✓	No	✓○	✖	No	✓	
Harris	BN	✖	✓	✓	No	✓	✓	Yes●	?	
Health Valley Nat. Foods#	HVAL	?	✓	✓	No	?	?	No	✓	
Health Valley	HVAL	?	✓	✓	No	?	?	No	✖	
Hearty Soup	UN	✖	✓	✓	No	✓*	✖	Yes†	?	
Hiltons	BN	✖	✓	✓	No	✓	✓	Yes●	✓	

✓ = Top Rating ✓ = Middle Rating ✖ = Bottom Rating ? = Insufficient Information
For a more detailed explanation see key on page 10

SOUP

Company or Product	Abbr.	#	♀	(minority)	(military)	(community)	(person)	(nuclear)	(flags)	(family)	ALERT
Home Cookin' Soup	CPB	✓	✓	✓	No	✓	✓	No	✓	✓	on-site daycare
Knorr	CPC	✗	✓	✓	No	?	✓	No	✓	✓	
Le Gout	K	✓	✓	✓	No	✓	✓	Yes●	✓	✓	
Lipton	UN	✗	✓	✓	No	✓*	✗	Yes†	?	?	
Lots-A-Noodles	UN	✗	✓	✓	No	✓*	✗	Yes†	?	?	
Mariner's Cove	CBI	✓	✓	?	No	✓	✓	No	?	✓	
Mayacamas#	MAYA	?	?	?	No	✓	✗	No	?	✗	
New Mill	BN	✗	✓	✓	No	✓	✓	Yes●	✓	✓	
Pepperidge Farm	CPB	✓	✓	✓	No	?	✓	No	?	✓	on-site daycare
Progresso Soup	WH	✓	✓	✓	No	✓○	✓	No	?	✓	
Redding Ridge Farms	UN	✗	✓	✓	No	✓*	✗	Yes†	?	?	
Snow's	BN	✗	✓	✓	No	✓	✓	No●	✓	✓	

Company or Product	Abbr.	💲	♀			⚛			ALERT
Soup Starter	BN	✗	✓	✓	No	No	✓	✓	
Soup Di Pasta	AHP	✗	✗	✓	No	Yes*	✓	✗	infant formula
Wyler's	BN	✗	✓	✓	No	Yes●	✓	✓	
SYRUPS & MOLASSES									
Aunt Jemima	OAT	✓	✓	✓	No	No	✓	✓	
Cary's	BN	✗	✓	✓	No	Yes●	✓	✓	
Country Kitchen	MO	✗	✓	✓	No	Yes	✗	?	cigarettes
Golden Griddle	CPC	✗	✓	✓	No	No	✓	✓	
Grandma's Molasses	CADB	✓	✗	✓	No	Yes†	?	✓	
Home Brands	CAG	?	?	✗	No	No	✓	?	OSHA fines

✓ = Top Rating   ✓ = Middle Rating   ✗ = Bottom Rating   ? = Insufficient Information
For a more detailed explanation see key on page 10

SYRUPS & MOLASSES

Company or Product	Abbr.	♀	$			No					ALERT
Karo	CPC	✗	✗	✓	✓	No	✓	No	✓	✓	
Log Cabin	MO	✗	✓	✓	✓	No	✓	Yes	✗	?	cigarettes
Lumber Jack	CBI	✓+	?	?	?	No	?	No	✓	✓	
Mrs. Butterworth's	UN	✗	✓	✓	✗	No	✓*	Yes†	✓	?	
Old Vermont	CAG	?	?	✓	✓	No	?	No	✓	?	OSHA fines
Smucker's	SJM	✓	✓	✗	✓	No	?	No	✓	✗	
Sunrise	G	?	?	✓	✓	No	?	No	✓	?	
Vermont Maid	RJR	✓	✓	✓	?	No	?	Yes*	✓	✗	cigarettes
TEA											
Banquets	MCRK	✓+	?	✓	✓	No	✓	No	✓	✗	
Celestial Seasonings	CS	?	✓	✓	?	No	✓	No	✓	✗	
Diner's Choice	K	✓	✓	✓	?	No	✓	Yes●	✓	✓	

Company or Product	Abbr.	💲	♀	✈	🌐	🪖	⚛	🐾	🕊	ALERT
Falcon Trading#	FALC	?	✓	No	✓	✓	No	No	✓	
Fruit Tea	MO	✗	✓	No	✓	✓	No	Yes	✗	cigarettes
Ice Teasers	NEST	?	?	No	✓	✗	No	Yes†	✓	infant formula
Lipton	UN	✗	✓	No	✓*	✗	No	Yes†	?	
Lyons	ALP	?	?	No	✓	?	No	Yes†	?	
Natura#	NFS	?	?	No	✓	✗	No	No	?	
Nestea	NEST	?	?	No	✓	✓	No	Yes†	✓	infant formula
T-Time	CADB	✓	✗	No	✓	✓	No	Yes†	✓	
Tea House	MCRK	✓+	?	No	✗	?	No	No	✗	
Tetley	ALP	?	?	No	✓	✗	No	Yes†	?	

✓ = Top Rating   ✓ = Middle Rating   ✗ = Bottom Rating   ? = Insufficient Information

For a more detailed explanation see key on page 10

TEA

VEGETABLES, CANNED

Company or Product	Abbr.	💲	⚥	👥	✈	🗺	⚛	🐾					ALERT
B 'n B	GMP	?	✓+	?	?	?	✗	?	?	Yes†	?	?	dolphins caught
Blue Boy	CBI	?	✓+	✓	No	?	✓	✓	No	No	?	✓	
Comstock	CBI	?	✓+	✓	No	?	✓	✓	No	No	?	✓	
Contadina	NEST	?	?	?	No	?	✓	✗	No	Yes†	?	✓	infant formula
Cortland Valley	CBI	?	✓+	✓	No	?	✓	✓	No	No	?	✓	
Countryside	HRL	?	✓	✓	No	✗	✓	✗	No	No	✓	✗	labor disputes
Del Monte	RJR	?	✓	✓	No	?	✓	?	No	Yes*	✗	✗	cigarettes
Early California	CPB	?	✓	✓	No	✓	✓	✓	No	No	✓	✓	on-site daycare
Eden#	EDEN	✗	✗	✗	No	✓	✓	✗	No	No	✓	✗	
Emerald Cove#	GES	?	?	✓	No	✓	✓	✓	No	No	✓	✗	
Farm Kitchen	BTC	?	✓+	✓	No	?	✓	?	No	No	?	✓	

Company or Product	Abbr.	💲				✈			⚛				ALERT
Green Giant	GMP	?	?	?	?	?	×	?	?	Yes†	?	?	dolphins caught
Hunt's	BTC	✔+	✔	?	?	✔	?	?	No	?	✔		
Le Seur Brand	GMP	?	?	?	?	?	×	?	?	Yes†	?	?	dolphins caught
Princella	GMP	?	?	?	?	?	×	?	?	Yes†	?	?	dolphins caught
Progresso	WH	✔	?	✔	No	✔⊙	✔	✔	No	No	✔		
Royal Prince	GMP	?	?	?	?	?	×	?	?	Yes†	?	?	dolphins caught
Thank You Brand	CBI	✔+	✔	?	No	?	✔	?	No	?	✔		
Van Camp's	OAT	✔	✔	✔	No	✔	✔	?	No	?	✔		
Victor	CBI	✔+	?	?	No	✔	✔	?	No	?	✔		
White Rose	DIG	?	?	?	No	✔	?	?	No	?	×		

✔ = Top Rating ✔ = Middle Rating ✖ = Bottom Rating ? = Insufficient Information

For a more detailed explanation see key on page 10

Page 231

VEGETABLES, CANNED

Company or Product	Abbr.	$	♀	✈	⚙	⚛	🐾	🕊	ALERT
YOGURT									
Breakstone's	MO	✖	✔	No	✔	✔	No	Yes	?	cigarettes
Breyers	MO	✖	✔	No	✔	✔	No	Yes	?	cigarettes
Brown Cow West#	BCWC	?	?	No	✔	✖	No	No	✔	
Dean	DF	?	?	No	✔	✖	No	No	✖	
Light n' Lively	MO	✖	✔	No	✔	✔	No	Yes	?	cigarettes
Mountain High	BN	✖	✔	No	✔	✔	No	Yes●	✔	
Sealtest	MO	✖	✔	No	✔	✔	No	Yes	✖	cigarettes
Stay 'n Shape	MO	✖	✔	No	✔	✔	No	Yes	?	cigarettes
Whitney's	K	✔	✔	No	✔	✔	No	Yes●	✔	

YOUR OWN WORKSHEET

Rate your own employer (any change from year to year?):

	1989									
1989										
1990										
1991										

How does your employer compare to other companies in the same industry?

Competitor 1:									
Competitor 2:									
Competitor 3:									

Where should your company focus its social concerns?

✔ = Top Rating   ◌ = Middle Rating   ✖ = Bottom Rating   ? = Insufficient Information

For a more detailed explanation see key on page 10

Page 233

WORKSHEET

America's Corporate Conscience Awards

Each year, The Council on Economic Priorities (CEP) presents its America's Corporate Conscience Awards. Corporations receive awards for their exemplary achievements in such areas as environmental responsibility, employer responsiveness, charitable contributions, equal opportunity, and community action. Nominations by CEP's Nominating Committee are also made for dishonorable mentions that highlight specific examples of corporate irresponsibility.

Based on the format used for the Academy Awards, a Blue Ribbon Panel of Judges choose the winners which are then announced at an annual dinner held in New York City. A cast of celebrities such as Dr. Ruth Westheimer, the Today Show's Jane Pauley, and Joanne Woodward, are also chosen to present the awards to corporate CEO's. Last year, 50 corporations and some 400 people participated in the Third Annual America's Corporate Conscience Awards.

To submit a nomination, contact CEP for a nomination packet. Individuals or corporations wishing to receive an invitation to the annual awards program may also contact CEP directly.

1989 Award Winners:

Charitable Contributions	Dayton Hudson
Employer Responsivenesss	Federal Express
Equal Opportunity	Eastman Kodak Company
Environment	Applied Energy Services
Community Action	Digital Equipment Corp.
Honorable Mentions	Newman's Own H.B. Fuller
Dishonorable Mentions	E.I. du Pont de Nemours & Company John Morrell & Co.

1988 Award Winners:

Charitable Contributions . Ben & Jerry's Homemade, Inc.

Community Action . . . . . Best Western International, Inc.
South Shore Bank

Fair Employment for Minorities . . . . . . Xerox Corporation

Fair Employment for Women . . . . Gannett Company

Family Concerns . . . . IBM Corporation

Opportunities for the Disabled . . . . General Mills, Inc.

Animal Rights . . . . Proctor & Gamble

Environment 3M

Education . . . . Gannett Company

Honorable Mention,

Corporate Disclosure . . . . Kellogg

Dishonorable Mentions . . . . Motron Thiokol
RJR Nabisco

1987 Award Winners:

Charitable Contributions . . . . General Mills, Inc.
Polaroid Corporation
Sara Lee Corporation

Community Action . . . . IBM Corporation
Amoco

Personnel & Family Concerns . . . . Proctor & Gamble

Fair Employment,

Women and Minorities . . . . Avon Products, Inc.

Honorable Mentions,

South Africa . . . . Polaroid Corporation

Corporate Disclosure . . . . Ford Motor Company
Johnson & Johnson

Dishonorable Mentions . . . . A.H. Robins
Mobil
American Cyanamid
Litton Industries

ALERT GLOSSARY

1st to Ban CFCs — In 1975, the National Academy of Sciences found a possible link between fluorocarbons and depletion of the earth's protective ozone layer. Samuel C. Johnson, president of S.C. Johnson & Son, was concerned and announced that the company would no longer use fluorocarbons in its aerosol spray cans. Johnson urged other companies to follow suit, but it was not until 1978, when the EPA banned fluorocarbons and chlorofluorocarbons (CFCs) for use as propellants in most aerosol sprays, that most other companies stopped using the chemicals. CFCs are still used as refrigerants, in plastic foams, to clean electronic components and in two percent of aerosols (those necessary in medical and pharmaceutical products). However, substitute chemicals are currently being researched and most major users of CFCs have announced they will phase out the chemicals' use in manufacturing. The timetables for the phase-outs vary from company to company.

1% for Peace — 1% For Peace, Inc. is a non-profit, non-partisan, national organization whose purpose is to create, promote and fund a positive peace agenda. One of the campaign's many goals is to pass a federal law requiring that 1% of the $300 billion defense budget (i.e. $3 billion) be redirected to peace through understanding.

cigarettes — These addictive products are made by three cigarette manufacturers that CEP studied for this guide. The companies are: Philip Morris, RJR Nabisco, and American Brands.

clearcutting — Of all the methods of logging, this is the cheapest, easiest and most destructive, as *all* trees in a given section are cut down. Clearcutting often results in heavy soil erosion since the protection of the trees is gone. Old-growth forests, where the trees are over 200 years old and cannot be replaced, are also devastated.

disposable diapers — Single-use diapers, introduced in 1962, are marketed as a way to revolutionize child care, freeing parents from the chores of diaper washing, rinsing, hanging and folding. But these plastic disposables raise many serious questions: they can remain intact for up to 500 years; little is known about the health effects of tossing diapers still containing urine and feces into garbage cans and landfills. Disposable diapers have become a symbol of our penchant for using disposable products that are more expensive and more harmful to the environment then re-usable products. They now make up 2% of our municipal solid waste. Procter & Gamble and Kimberly-Clark control 80% of the disposable diaper market in this country, a $3.3 billion-a-year industry.

dolphins caught — In the eastern tropical Pacific, schools of yellowfin tuna often swim together with dolphins. Some fishing boats follow the dolphins and lower mile-long nets, encircling both dolphins and tuna. Although the dolphins are supposed to be released alive, the U.S. Government estimates that more than 100,000 are killed each year. Since this method of tuna fishing began in the 1960s, it has led to the needless deaths of over 6 million dolphins, according to Earth Island Institute in San Francisco. As a result, certain species of dolphins are now endangered; if the tuna companies do not mend their ways the dolphins may become extinct. Nearly 95% of all tuna is caught without harming dolphins. Thus an end to the killing would not cause tuna shortages or shut down the U.S. tuna fleet. Three species of tuna — bonito, skipjack and albacore — are not caught in association with the dolphins. However, bonito and skipjack are packaged with yellowfin and sold as "light meat" or "chunk light". Albacore or "white" tuna is not mixed with the yellowfin.

forestry criticized — Scott Paper Company is being boycotted for its forestry practices in Nova Scotia. The Scott Boycott Committee charges Scott with using highly-destructive clearcutting and dangerous insecticides and herbicides. The company is alleged to have repeatedly violated spraying guidelines for these chemicals. Scott's policy of replanting clear-cut areas with monoculture — softwood forests which are highly susceptible to insect outbreaks — has also come under criticism by the boycott committee. Scott denies the boycotters' charges, maintaining that its forestry practices are outstanding for the area and have been cited as model programs.

heart-valve suit — Bjork-Shiley (a subsidiary of Pfizer Corp.) manufactured a prosthetic heart between the years 1979 and 1986, when it was withdrawn due to a small percentage of reported strut fractures. Over 80,000 of these valves have been implanted in patients around the world. According to the Public Citizen Health Research Group in Washington, the number of deaths reported due to the alleged defect in the valves had risen to 180 by May 1988. Pfizer has resolved a number of cases related to the heart-valve through out-of-court settlements.

INFACT boycott — INFACT is a grassroots action organization whose campaigns attempt to hold corporations directly accountable for their practices that endanger the health and survival of people around the world. On June 12, 1986, INFACT initiated a boycott of the highly visible General Electric Corporation for its instrumental role in promoting and producing nuclear weapons. In 1988, G.E. received $3.4 billion in contracts from the Departments of Energy and Defense for nuclear weapons systems. The boycott is estimated to have 3 million supporters.

infant formula — The morality and legality of corporate donations of infant formula as breast milk substitutes to Third World hospitals has been questioned for years. These free or subsidized samples are used as a marketing tool by the companies. The health implications can be severe. If breast feeding is stopped in the early stages of post-natal care the production of breast milk ceases. When she leaves the hospital the mother, now dependent on the costly formula, may mix it with contaminated water or dilute it to make it last longer. These practices often result in Bottle Baby Disease which can lead to death. In 1981, the World Health Organization and UNICEF set up an international code to regulate the marketing of breast milk substitutes. While the companies maintain that they are not in violation of this code, certain groups, like ACTION for Corporate Accountability, disagree and have organized boycotts. Nestle and American Home Products have been targetted by these boycotts, but other American companies employ similar practices.

labor disputes — Hormel recently came to an agreement with the new United Food and Commercial Workers (UFCW) Local at their plant in Austin, Minnesota. Members of the old Local P-9 union assert that the UFCW union is made up primarily of scabs and has done almost nothing to meet their concerns. Former P-9 members continue their boycott of Hormel in order to force the company to address worker safety concerns, return the jobs of laid-off workers, and bring an end to the repeated concessions imposed on workers. United Brands' labor disputes result mainly from problems at its John Morrell subsidiary. Members of UFCW Locals, as well as the UFCW International and the AFL-CIO, have called for a boycott of Morrell. They contend that Morrell has repeatedly forced major concessions upon its workers and has increased the speed of its production line, resulting in a dramatic increase of injuries. In October, 1988 the Occupational Safety and Health Administisitration (OSHA) proposed a $4.3 million fine for alleged safety and health violations at Morrell's Sioux Falls, S.D. plant. The company is contesting the charges.

makes/uses pesticides — Company makes or uses pesticides, which are used to kill the natural enemies of certain foods and crops. These chemicals can cause a number of problems. Many are washed by rainwater from farmland into rivers and streams; they can be harmful and sometimes fatal to farmworkers applying them without proper protection; their residues may remain on and in fruits and vegetables; and they have in some cases even made their intended targets immune so that more and stronger chemicals must be used. Of the 316 pesticides registered with the EPA, current testing methods at the FDA can detect only 163. Alternative organic and biological methods of dealing with foods' natural enemies are increasingly being used with successful results.

oil spill — The Good Friday, 1989 grounding of the tanker Exxon Valdez on a reef in Alaska's Prince William Sound resulted in the worst oil spill in U.S. history. Some 11 million gallons of oil spilled, washing up on over 400 miles of pristine Alaskan shoreline, killing and injuring thousands of otters, seals, fish and birds, and rivetting the nation's attention on the price oil-dependence exacts on our environment. Investigations into the tragedy reveal a trail of broken oil industry promises for improved accident prevention and quick emergency response.

on-site day care — one of a relatively few U.S. corporations to offer child care at the workplace, Campbell Soup Company subsidizes 50 percent of the tuition for 110 children of its Camden, N.J. headquarters employees. It has also helped upgrade day care facilities overall in the Camden area.

OSHA fines — the Occupational Safety and Health Administration (OSHA) is the division of the U.S. Department of Labor charged with regulating corporate health and safety practices. ConAgra was cited for inaccuracies in the documentation of injury and illness records. The company is alleged to have subjected its workers to hazardous conditions, resulting in cumulative injuries.

profit to charity — Newman's Own, Inc. the all-natural food company founded by actor Paul Newman, has donated all its profits (total $22 million since 1982) to charitable causes. Notable among the 400 organizations that it donates to is the Hole-in-the-Wall Gang Camp for children with life-threatening diseases. In this program, the children are given the chance the enjoy the outdoors. Ordinarily they spend much of their lives in the hospital. The camp charges no fees.

refuses cans — Several New York City supermarkets were sued in 1989 for turning away poor and homeless people who attempted to return large numbers of bottles and cans. State bottle-return laws mandate that supermarkets accept up to 240 containers per person per day. The supermarkets claimed the laws resulted in an economic hardship for them. But the court ruled against the stores, saying the homeless were being ''deprived of funds they desperately need.'' The stores were: D'Agostino, A&P, Food Emporium, Gristede's, Red Apple, Shopwell, and Sloan's.

removed tobacco — In 1988, Vons Companies Inc., the largest supermarket chain in Southern California, removed all cigars, pipes and chewing tobacco from its shelves because the companies that make the products failed to put consumer warning labels on them. ''Clear and reasonable warnings'' on all products which expose consumers to chemicals known to cause cancer or birth defects are required by California's Proposition 65 referendum, passed in 1986. The stores continue to sell cigarettes, which already carry Federal health warnings.

worst plant for air — Texaco's Chemical plant in Port Neches on Texas' Gulf Coast was cited in 1989 by the EPA as the country's worst air pollution risk. Nearby residents, according to the report, face a one-in-ten risk of cancer from emissions of butadiene (an odorless gas used in the production of synthetic rubber). A one-in-ten risk means that one person in ten would contract cancer if exposed to the chemical for eight hours per day over 70 years. Texaco disputed the report, stating that a company analysis found emissions 40 percent lower than the EPA reported.

COMPANY ADDRESSES

Many consumers who purchased the 1989 edition of **SHOPPING FOR A BETTER WORLD** told us they would like the addresses, phone numbers, and names of chief officers of the companies included in the guide. Here they are. Write to the companies and tell them why you have changed your buying habits.

21st Century Foods, Inc. #
30 A Germania St.
Jamaica Plain, MA 02130
(617) 522-7595
Rudy Canale, Owner

A&P (Great Atlantic & Pacific Tea Company)
2 Paragon Drive
Montvale, NJ 07645
(201) 573-9700
James Wood, Chairman & CEO

Abbott Laboratories
One Abbott Park Road
Abbott Park, IL 60064-3500
(312) 937-6100
Robert A. Schoelhorn, Chairman & CEO

Alberto Culver
2525 Armitage Avenue
Melrose Park, IL 60160
(312) 450-3000
Leonard H. Lavin, Chairman & CEO

Albertson's Inc.
250 Parkcenter Blvd., Box 20
Boise, ID 83726
(208) 385-6200
Warren E. McCain, Chairman & CEO

Allied-Lyons PLC.
Allied House
156 St. John St.
London EC1 PLAR ¡ United Kingdom
Sir Derrick Holden-Brown, Chairman & CEO

American Brands, Inc.
1700 East Putnam Ave., P.O. Box 811
Old Greenwich, CT 06870-0811
(203) 698-5000
William J. Alley, Chairman & CEO

American Cyanamid Company
One Cyanamid Plaza
Wayne, NJ 07470
(201) 831-2000
George J. Sella, Chairman & CEO

American Health Products #
70 Hilltop Road
Ramsey, NJ 07446
(914) 735-0640
Reynald M. Swift, President

American Home Products
685 Third Avenue
New York, NY 10017-4085
(212) 878-5000
John R. Stafford, Chairman & CEO

American Stores
5201 Amelia Earhart Drive
Salt Lake City, UT 84116
(801) 539-0112
Jonathan L. Scott, Vice Chairman & CEO

Amoco Corporation
200 East Randolph Drive
Chicago, IL 60601
(312) 856-6111
Richard M. Morrow, Chairman & CEO

Anheuser-Busch Companies, Inc.
One Busch Place
St. Louis, MO 63118
(314) 577-2000
August A. Busch III, Chairman & President

Apple & Eve #
P.O. Box 2137
Great Neck, NY 11022
(516) 829-6881
Gordon Crance, President

Archer Daniels Midland Company
P.O. Box 1470
Decatur, IL 62525
(217) 424-5200
Dwayne O. Andreas, Chairman & CEO

Aroma Vera #
2728 So. Robertson Blvd.
Los Angeles, CA 90034
(213) 280-0407
Marcel Lavabre, President

Arrowhead Mills, Inc. #
P.O. Box 2059
Hereford, TX 79045
(806) 364-0730
Boyd M. Foster, President & CEO

Associated Cooperatives #
322 Harbour Way, Suite 25
Richmond, CA 94801
(415) 232-1111
Terry Baird, General Mgr.

Atlantic Richfield (ARCO)
515 South Flower Street
Los Angeles, CA 90071
(213) 486-3511
Lodwrick M. Cook, Chairman & CEO

Aubrey Organics #
4419 N. Manhattan Ave.
Tampa, FL 33614
(813) 877-4186
Aubrey Hampton, CEO

Aura Cacia #
1302 Nugget Lane (P.O. Box 391)
Weaverville, CA 96093
(916) 623-3301
Doug Nowacki, President

Autumn Harp #
28 Rockydale Rd.
Bristol, UT 05443
(806) 453-4807
Kevin Harper, President

Avon Products, Inc.
9 West 57th Street
New York, NY 10019
(212) 546-6015
James E. Preston, Chairman & CEO

Barbara's Bakery #
3900 Cypress Drive
Petaluma, CA 94952
(707) 765-2273
Gil Pritchard, President & CEO

Beatrice Company
Two North LaSalle Street
Chicago, IL 60602
(312) 558-4000
Fred Rentschler, CEO

Beecham Group PLC
Beecham House
Brentford, Middlesex TW89 BD
United Kingdom
Robert P. Bauman, Chairman

Ben & Jerry's
Route 100
P.O. Box 240
Waterbury, VT 05676
(802) 244-5641
Fred Lager, President

Borden, Inc.
277 Park Ave.
New York, NY 10172
(212) 573-4000
R.J. Ventres, Chairman & CEO

BP America, Inc.
200 Public Square
Cleveland, OH 44114
(216) 586-4141
James H. Ross, President & CEO

Bristol-Myers
345 Park Avenue
New York, NY 10154
(212) 546-4000
Richard L. Gelb, Chairman & CEO

Brown Cow West Corporation #
190 Seely Hill Rd.
Newfield, NY 14867
(607) 564-9928
Tom Gerhart, President

Bruno's Inc.
300 Research Parkway
Birmingham, AL 35211
(205) 940-9400
Angelo J. Bruno, Chairman

H.E. Butt Grocery
646-G S. Main Ave., Box 9999
San Antonio, TX 78204-0999
(512) 270-8000
Charles C. Butt, President & CEO

Cadbury Schweppes, Inc.
High Ridge Park
Stamford, CT 06905-0800
(203) 329-0911
James P. Schadt, President & CEO

Campbell Soup
Campbell Place
Camden, NJ 08103-1799
(609) 342-4800
William S. Cashel, Jr., Chairman & CEO

Carme
84 Galli Drive
Novato, CA 94947
(415) 883-3367
James A. Egide, President

Carter-Wallace
767 Fifth Avenue
New York, NY 10153
(212)758-4500
Henry H. Hoyt, Jr., CEO

Castle & Cooke, Inc.
10900 Wilshire Boulevard
Los Angeles, CA 90024
(213) 824-1500
David H. Murdock, Chairman & CEO

Celestial Seasonings
1780 55th Street
Boulder, CO 80301-2799
(303) 449-3779
Barney Feinblum, President

Cherry Hill Cooperative #
MR # 1
Barre, VT 05641
(802) 479-2558
Ken Davis, Manager

Chevron
225 Bush Street
San Francisco, CA 94104
(415) 894-7700
George M. Keller, CEO

Church & Dwight
489 North Harrison Street
Princeton, NJ 08540
(609) 683-5900
Dwight C. Minton, Chairman & CEO

The Clorox Company
1221 Broadway
Oakland, CA 94612
(415) 271-7000
C.R. Weaver, Chairman & CEO

Coca-Cola Company
P.O. Drawer 1734
Atlanta, GA 30301
(404) 676-2121
Roberto C. Goizueta, Chairman & CEO

Colgate-Palmolive Company
300 Park Avenue
New York, NY 10022
(212) 310-2000
Reuben Mark, Chairman & CEO

ConAgra, Inc.
ConAgra Center
One Central Park Plaza
Omaha, NE 68102
(402) 978-4000
Charles M. Harper, Chairman & CEO

Coors Co., Adolph
NH-325
Golden, CO 80401
(303) 279-6565
William K. Coors, Chairman

CPC International
P.O. Box 8000, International Plaza
Englewood Cliffs, NJ 07632
(201) 894-4000
James R. Eiszner, Chairman & CEO

Curtice-Burns Foods, Inc.
One Lincoln First Square, P.O. Box 681
Rochester, NY 14603
(716) 325-1020
Ralph E. Winsor, Chairman

Dean Foods Company
3600 North River Rd.
Franklin Park, IL 60131
(312) 678-1680
Howard M. Dean, President & CEO

Deer Valley Farm #
Rd # 1 Co. Rt. 37
Guilford, NY 13780
(607) 764-8556
Robert Carsten, President

Di Giorgio Corporation
One Maritime Plaza
San Francisco, CA 94111
(415) 765-0100
Peter F. Scott, Chairman & CEO

Dolefam #
2000 K Street
Washington, DC 20006
(202) 775-9715
Vincent Dole, President

Dominick's Finer Foods
505 Railroad Ave.
Northlake, IL 60164
(312) 562-1000
Dan Josephs, President

Dow Chemical Company
2030 Willard H. Dow Center
Midland, MI 48674
(517) 636-1000
Frank P. Popoff, President & CEO

Eastman Kodak Company
343 State Street
Rochester, NY 14650
(716) 724-4000
Colby H. Chandler, Chairman & CEO

Eden Foods #
701 Tecumseh Rd.
Clinton, MI 49236
(313) 973-9400
Michael Potter, President

Exxon Corporation
1251 Avenue of the Americas
New York, NY 10020-1198
(212) 333-1000
L.G. Rawl, Chairman

Faberge, Inc.
Trump Tower - 17th Floor
725 Fifth Avenue
New York, NY 10022
(212) 735-9300
Daniel J. Manella, CEO

Falcon Trading Co. #
1055 17th Ave.
Santa Cruz, CA 95062
(408) 462-1280
Morty Cohen, President

Fantastic Foods, Inc. #
106 Galli Drive
Novato, CA 94949
(415) 883-7718
James Rosen, President

First Brands
83 Wooster Heights Rd. Bldg. 301
P.O. Box 1911
Danbury, CT 06813-1911
(203) 731-2318
Alfred E. Dudley, President & CEO

Flowers Industries, Inc.
U.S. Highway 19
P.O. Box 1338
Thomasville, GA 31792
(912) 226-9110
Amos R. McMullian, Chairman & CEO

Food Lion
P.O. Box 1330
2110 Executive Dr.
Salisbury, NC 28145-1330
(704) 633-8250
Tom E. Smith, CEO

Fred Meyer, Inc.
3800 SE 22nd Ave.
Portland, OR 97202
(503) 232-8844
Frederick M. Stevens, Chairman & CEO

Garden of Eatin' #
5300 Santa Monica Blvd.
Los Angeles, CA 90029
(213) 462-5406
Al H. Jacobson, President

General Electric
3135 Eastern Turnpike
Fairfield, CT 06431
(203) 373-2431
John F. Welch, Jr., Chairman & CEO

General Mills
Number One General Mills Blvd.
P.O. Box 1113
Minneapolis, MN 55440
(612) 540-2311
H.B. Atwater, Jr., Chairman & CEO

Georgia-Pacific Corporation
133 Peachtree Street, N.E.
P.O. Box 105605
Atlanta, GA 30303
(404) 521-4000
T. Marshall Hahn, Jr., Chairman & CEO

Gerber Products
445 State Street
Fremont, MI 49412
(616) 928-2000
David W. Johnson, Chairman & CEO

Giant Eagle, Inc.
RIDC Industrial Pk.
Pittsburgh, PA 15238
(412) 963-6200
David Shapira, CEO

Giant Food Inc.
6300 Sheriff Road
Landover, MD 20785
(301) 341-4100
Israel Cohen, CEO

The Gillette Company
Prudential Tower Building
Boston, MA 02199
(617) 421-7000
Colman M. Mockler, Jr., Chairman

Grand Metropolitan PLC
11-12 Hanover Sq.
London W1A 1DP, United Kingdom
(01) 629-7488
Allen Sheppard, CEO

Grand Union Company
201 Willowbrook Blvd.
Wayne, NJ 07470
(201) 890-6000
Floyd Hall, CEO

Great Eastern Sun #
92 McIntosh Rd.
Asheville, NC 28806
(704) 252-3090
Bob Ballard, President

The Greyhound Corporation
Greyhound Tower
Phoenix, AZ 85077
(602) 248-4000
John W. Teets, Chairman, President & CEO

GTE Corporation
One Stamford Forum
Stamford, CT 06904
(203) 965-2000
Theodore F. Brophy, Chairman & CEO

Health Valley Natural Foods #
16100 Foothill Blvd.
Irwindale, CA 91706-7811
(800) 423-4846
George Mateljan, Jr., President

H.J. Heinz Company
P.O. Box 57
Pittsburgh, PA
(412) 456-5700
Anthony O'Reilly, Chairman, President & CEO

Hershey Food Corporation
100 Mansion Road East
Hershey, PA 17033
(717) 534-4000
Richard Zimmerman, Chairman & CEO

Holly Farms Corporation
P.O. Box 17236
Memphis, TN 38187-0236
(901) 761-3610
R. Lee Taylor, President & CEO

Homestyle Foods #
2317 Bluebell Dr.
Santa Rosa, CA 95403
(707) 525-8822
Robert Dolgin, President

Hormel, George A. & Company
P.O. Box 800
Austin, MN 55912
(507) 437-5737
R.L. Knowlton, Chairman, President & CEO

Imagine Foods #
299 California Ave. # 305
Palo Alto, CA 94306
(415) 327-1444
Robert Nissenbaum, President

Iroquois Brands
20405 F.M. 249, Suite 700
Houston, TX 77070
(713) 320-8593
Malcolm H. Stockdale, CEO

James River Corporation
P.O. Box 2218
Richmond, VA 23217
(804) 644-5411
Brenton S. Halsey, Chairman & CEO

Johnson & Johnson
1 Johnson & Johnson Plaza
New Brunswick, NJ 08933
(201) 524-0400
James E. Burke, Chairman & CEO

S.C. Johnson & Son, Inc.
1525 Howe Street
Racine, WI 54303-5011
(414) 631-2121
Samuel C. Johnson, Chairman & CEO

Johnson Products Co., Inc.
8522 South Lafayette Avenue
Chicago, IL 60620
(312) 483-4100
George E. Johnson, President & CEO

Kanoa: A Free Spirit #
11325 First Ave.
Pleasant Prairie, WI 53158
(414) 697-0548
Kimberly A. Gorham, Comptroller

Kellogg Company
One Kellogg Square, P.O. Box 3599
Battle Creek, MI 49016-3599
(616) 961-2000
William E. LaMothe, Chairman & CEO

Kimberly-Clark Corporation
P.O. Box 619100, DFW Airport Station
Dallas, TX 75261-9100
(214) 830-1200
Darwin E. Smith, Chairman & CEO

Klaire Labs #
1573 W. Seminole
San Marcos, CA 92069
(619) 744-9680
Claire Farr, President

The Kroger Company
1014 Vine Street
Cincinnatti , OH 45201
(513) 762-4000
Lyle Everingham, Chairman & CEO

Lifetone International #
One S. Ocean Blvd.
Boca Raton, FL 33432
(407) 391-1611
George Schrenzel, President

Loma Linda Foods
11503 Pierce Street
Riverside, CA 92515
(714) 687-7800
Alejo Pizarro, President

Loriva Supreme Foods
P.O. Box 871
Smithtown, NY 11787
(516) 231-7940
William S. Robertson, President

Mars Inc.
6885 Elm Street
McLean, VA 22101
(703) 821-4900
Forrest E. Mars, Co-President

Mayacamas Fine Foods #
1206 East MacArthur
Sonoma, CA 95476
(707) 996-0955
Ross W. Webber, President

McCormick & Company, Inc.
11350 McCormick Road
Hunt Valley, MD 21031
(301) 771-7301
Charles P. McCormick, Jr., Chairman & CEO

The Mead Corporation
World Headquarters
Court House Plaza Northeast
Dayton, OH 45463
(513) 495-3428
Burnell R. Roberts, Chairman & CEO

Miles Laboratories
1127 Myrtle Street
Elkhart, IN 46515
(219) 264-8111
Klaus H. Risse, Ph.D., President & CEO

Minnesota Mining And Manufacturing Company (3M)
3M Center
St. Paul, MN 55144-1000
(612) 733-1110
Allen F. Jacobson, Chairman & CEO

Mobil Corporation
150 East 42nd Street
New York, NY 10017-5666
(212) 883-4242
Allen E. Murray, Chairman & CEO

Modern Products #
3015 W. Vera Ave.
Milwaukee, WI 53209
(414) 352-3208
Anthony Palermo, CEO

Mountain Ocean #
Box 951
Boulder, CO 80306
(303) 444-2751
Tom Benjamin, President

Murdock International
10 Mountain Spring Parkway
Springville, UT 84663
(801) 489-3635
Ken Murdock, President

Natura Foods #
30596 San Antonia St.
Hayward, CA 94544
(415) 487-1729
Donald Sakiyama, President

Nature's Herbs #
1113 N. Industrial Park Rd.
Orem, UT 84057
(801) 225-4443
Paul Larsen, President

Nestle S.A.
CH-1800
Vevey, Switzerland

Newman's Own, Inc. #
246 Post Road East
Westport, CT 06880
(203) 222-0136
Paul Newman, President

Noxell Corporation
11050 York Road
Hunt Valley, MD 21030-2098
(301) 785-7300
George L. Bunting, Chairman & CEO

Ocean Spray Cranberries, Inc.
225 Water St.
Lakeville/Middleboro, MA 02346
(508) 946-1000
John S. Llewellyn, Jr., President & CEO

Orjene Natural Cosmetics #
5-43 48th Avenue
Long Island City, NY 11101
(718) 937-2666
Gene Gomory, President

Paul Penders #
2810 E. Long St.
Tampa, FL 33605
(813) 248-6640
Paul Penders, President

PepsiCo, Inc.
Anderson Hill Road
Purchase, NY 10577
(914) 253-2000
D. Wayne Calloway, Chairman & CEO

Pfizer Inc.
235 East 42nd Street
New York, NY 10017
(212) 573-2323
Edmund T. Pratt, Chairman & CEO

Philip Morris Companies, Inc.
120 Park Avenue
New York, NY 10017
(212) 880-5000
Hamish Maxwell, Chairman & CEO

Phillips Petroleum Company
Phillips Building
Bartlesville, OK 74004
(918) 661-6600
C.J. Silas, President & CEO

Polaroid
549 Technology Square
Cambridge, MA 02139
(617) 577-2000
Robert E. Cawthorn, CEO

The Procter & Gamble Company
1 Procter & Gamble Plaza
Cincinatti, OH 45202-3315
(513) 983-2342
John G. Smale, Chairman & CEO

Publix Super Markets
P.O. Box 407
Lakeland, FL 33802-0407
(813) 688-1188
R. William Schroter, Vice President

The Quaker Oats Company
321 North Clark Street
Chicago, IL 60610
(312) 222-7111
William D. Smithburg, Chairman & CEO

Rachel Perry #
9111 Mason Ave.
Chatsworth, CA 91311
(818) 888-5881
Rachel Perry, President

Ralph's Grocery Company
1100 West Artesia Boulevard
Compton, CA 90220
(213) 637-1101
Byron Allumbaugh, Chairman

Ralston Purina Company
Checkerboard Square
St. Louis, MO 63164
(314) 982-1000
William P. Stiritz, Chairman & CEO

Reviva Labs #
705 Hopkins Rd.
Haddonfield, NJ 08033
(609) 428-3885
Stephen Strassler, President

Revlon Group, Inc.
21 East 63rd Street
New York, NY 10021
(212) 593-4300
Ronald Perelman, Chairman & CEO

Reynold's Metals Company
6601 West Broad Street
Richmond, VA 23261
(804) 281-2000
William O. Bourke, Chairman & CEO

RJR Nabisco
9 West 57th St. 48th Fl.
New York, NY 10022
Louis V. Gerstner, President & CEO

Rorer Group Inc.
500 Virginia Dr.
Fort Washington, PA 19034
(215) 628-6800
Robert E. Cawthorn, CEO

Safeway Stores
Fourth and Jackson Streets
Oakland, CA 94660
(415) 891-3000
Peter A. Magowan, CEO

John B. Sanfilippo & Son
2299 Busse Rd.
Elk Grove Village, IL 60007
(312) 593-2300
Jasper Sanfilippo, President

San-J International #
2880 Sprouse Drive
Richmond, VA 23231
(415) 821-4041
John Perelman, V.P., Consumer Sales

Sara Lee Corporation
Three First National Plaza
Chicago, IL 60602-4260
(312) 726-2600
John H. Bryan, Jr., Chairman & CEO

Schering-Plough Corporation
One Giralda Farms
Madison, NJ 07940-1000
(201) 822-7000
Robert P. Luciano, Chairman & CEO

Scott Paper Company
Scott Plaza
Philadelphia, PA 19113
(215) 522-5000
Philip E. Lippincott, Chairman & CEO

The Seagram Company Ltd.
1430 Peel Street
Montreal, Quebec
Canada H3A 1S9
Edgar M. Bronfman, Chairman & CEO

Shell Oil Company, USA
1 Shell Plaza, P.O. Box 2463
Houston, TX 77252
(713) 241-4083
Frank H. Richardson, President & CEO

Smith's Food & Drug Centers, Inc.
1550 South Redwood Road, P.O. Box 30550
Salt Lake City, UT 84104
(801) 974-1494
Jeff Smith, CEO

J.M. Smucker Company
Strawberry Lane
Orrville, OH 44667
(216) 682-0015
Paul Smucker, Chairman & CEO

Solgar Co.
410 Ocean Ave.
Lynbrook, NY 11563
(516) 599-2442
Nathaniel Colby, President

Squibb Corporation
P.O. Box 4000
Princeton, NJ 08543-4000
(609) 921-4000
Richard M. Furland, Chairman & CEO

Stop & Shop Companies Inc.
P.O. Box 369
Boston, MA 02101
(617) 770-8000
Avram J. Goldberg, CEO

Sun Company
100 Matsonford Road
Radnor, PA 19087-4797
(215) 293-6000
Robert McClements, Jr., V.P.

Supermarkets General Holdings Corp.
200 Milik Street
Carteret, NJ 07008
(201) 499-3000
Kenneth Peskin, CEO

Tasty Baking Company
2801 Hunting Park Avenue
Philadelphia, PA 19129
(215) 221-8500
Nelson G. Harris, CEO

Texaco, Inc.
2000 Westchester Avenue
White Plains, NY 10650
(914) 253-4000
James W. Kinnean, President & CEO

Tillamook Cheese
Box 313
Tillamook, OR 97141
(503) 842-4481
D.R. Sutton, Manager

Tom's of Maine #
Railroad Avenue
Kennebunk, ME 04043
(207) 985-2944
Tom Chappell, President

Topps Chewing Gum Inc.
254 36th Street
Brooklyn, NY 11232
(718) 768-8900
Arthur T. Shorin, Chairman & CEO

Twin Laboratories
2120 Smithtown Ave.
Ronkonkoma, NY 11779
(516) 467-3140
David Blechman, President

Tyson Foods, Inc.
2219 West Oaklawn Drive
Springdale, AR 72764
(501) 756-4000
Don Tyson, Chairman & CEO

Unilever N.V.
P.O. Box 760 3000
DK Rotterdam
Netherlands
F.A. Maljers, Chairman

United Biscuits (Holdings) PLC
P.O. Box 40, Syan Lane
Isleworth, Middlesex TW7 SNN
United Kingdom
Sir Hector Laing, Chairman

United Brands
1 East Fourth Street
Cincinnati, OH 45202
(413) 579-2115
Carl Linderner, CEO

Universal Foods Corporations
433 East Michigan Street
Milwaukee, WI 53202
(414) 271-6755
John L. Murray, Chairman

Universal Labs #
3 Terminal Road
New Brunswick, NJ 08901
(201) 545-3130
Timothy Tantum, Sls. Mgr.

The Upjohn Company
7000 Portage Road
Kalamazoo, MI 49001
(616) 323-4000
Theodore Cooper, Chairman & CEO

USX Corporation
600 Grant Street
Pittsburgh, PA 15219-4776
(412) 433-1121
David M. Roderick, Chairman & CEO

Vegetarian Health #
P.O. Box 525
Haywood, IL 60513
(312) 547-1700
John Price, President & CEO

The Vons Companies, Inc.
10150 Lower Azusa Road
El Monte, CA 91731
(818) 579-1400
Roger E. Stangeland, Chairman & CEO

Warner-Lambert Company
201 Tabor Road
Morris Plains, NJ 07950
(201) 540-2000
Joseph D. Williams, Chairman & CEO

Whitman Corporation
One Illinois Center
111 East Wacker Drive
Chicago, IL 60601
(312) 565-3000
Karl D. Bays, Chairman & CEO

Wilson Foods Corp.
4545 N. Lincoln Blvd.
Oklahoma City, OK 73105
(405) 525-4545
Kenneth J. Griggy, CEO

Winn-Dixie Stores, Inc.
P.O. Box B
Jacksonville, FL 32203
(904) 783-5000
A. Dano Davis, Chairman

Wm. Wrigley Jr. Company
410 North Michigan Ave.
Chicago, IL 60611
(312) 644-2121
William Wrigley, President & CEO

DISCLAIMER

The ratings in this guide are based on information current as of August 1989 and in some instances earlier. The data were gathered from:

1) extensive data from the companies themselves
2) existing public information available in government agencies, libraries and specialized centers, or from citizens' groups, and
3) advisors who are experts in our chosen categories.

CEP claims no predictive value for its ratings; a company may change its behavior tomorrow.

CEP claims no knowledge of programs or problems not in the public domain or voluntarily submitted by the companies themselves or other sources.

CEP is a non-partisan organization which does not endorse any product or company. If a company receives a high rating it does not mean that we approve of all of its policies, it is merely a recognition of the company's accomplishments in that specific area. Our ratings apply to the company as a whole and do not purport to rate individual products. For such evaluations, we refer you to such sources as Consumers Union and The Center for Science in the Public Interest. Our ratings are based entirely on factual information, so it is up to each consumer to decide which companies he or she wants to support.

ABOUT THE RESEARCH

In preparing this guide, the Council on Economic Priorities used information gathered in several ways: 1) questionnaires filled out by the companies themselves, 2) printed material from, or phone interviews with, company officials, 3) specialized institutions such as the Center for Science in the Public Interest (DC), the Foundation Center (NY), the Data Center (CA), Investor Responsibility Research Center (DC), Interfaith Center on Corporate Responsibility (NY), Independent Sector (DC), Civitex (CO), Nuclear Free America (MD), American Committee on Africa (NY), National Women's Economic Alliance Foundation (DC), the Environmental Protection Agency (DC) and state and regional regulatory agencies, the Natural Resources Defense Council (NY), the Bureau of National Affairs (NY), Environmental Action Foundation (NY), Greenpeace (DC), Environmental Law Institute (DC), OMB Watch (DC), Working Committee on Community Right to Know (DC), and trade unions, 4) business and public libraries, especially for such resources as the Taft *Corporate Giving Directory* and the *National Data Book*, 5) government agencies, and 6) advisors who are experts in our various categories. (Please see page 269 for a complete list of advisors.) After months of research, we sent each company our ratings with a request for corrections and updates.

The Council looked for reasonably comprehensive, comparable data — a task that was far more difficult in some areas than in others. For example, definitive data is publicly available on South African involvement and Charitable Contributions, making these issues easier to compare. Categories such as Environment and Community Outreach are extremely complex, so that even with substantial information, data were not always comparable company to company. The reader should be aware that ratings in these two categories are less precise.

Much more publicly available information is needed, even in simpler-to-rate areas such as the advancement of women and minorities. Where firms cooperated with CEP's efforts by answering all or most of our survey, a more complete picture emerges. CEP would like to thank the cooperating companies for providing us with comprehensive information while some of their peers did not.

ADVISORS

Richard Adams
Director
New Consumer U.K.

Lindsay Audin
Energy Consultant

David R. Brower
Chairman
Earth Island Institute

Mary Camper-Titsingh
Proxy Analyst, Investments

James S. Cannon
Energy & Environmental Consultant

Maurice E. Culver
Executive Director
Project Equality, Inc.

Jerome L. Dodson
President
The Parnassus Fund

Albert Donnay
Nuclear Free America

Michael F. Jacobson, Ph.D.
Executive Director
Center for Science in the Public Interest

Gene R. LaRocque
Rear Admiral, USN (Ret.)
Director, Center for Defense Information

Steven D. Lydenberg
Research Associate
Franklin Research & Development

Michael Mariotte
Nuclear Information & Resource Service

Michael McCloskey,
Chairman
Sierra Club

Susan Meeker-Lowry
Catalyst

Susan Rich
Director, Compassion Campaign
People for the Ethical Treatment of Animals (PETA)

Stephen S. Ross
Assistant Professor, Columbia University
President, New Jersey Environmental Lobby

Robert J. Schwartz, Ph.D.
Treasurer
Economists Against the Arms Race

Joan Shapiro
Senior Vice President
The South Shore Bank of Chicago

Tim Smith
Executive Director
Interfaith Center on Corporate Responsibility

Henry Spira
Animal Rights International

Shopping For A Better World: The Next Step

Congratulations! By using **SHOPPING FOR A BETTER WORLD** to guide your shopping decisions, you (and over 300,000 others) have taken the first step towards casting your economic vote. But there are many other ways you, as a consumer, can make your voice heard. Here are just a few suggestions.

Letters to the Companies

Our research has shown that the Chief Executive Officer plays a major role in determining a company's commitment to social issues. Why not write to one directly? Explain what you like — or don't like — about their policies, practices or products. And if you've changed brands, tell both companies why. This is a message they'll hear loud and clear.

To help you do this, we've included the names and addresses of all the companies listed in **SHOPPING FOR A BETTER WORLD** (page 242). Here are two sample letters actually written by a consumer who bought **SHOPPING FOR A BETTER WORLD** last year:

(Letter to William Wrigley Jr. Co.)

"Today I have decided to break a long habit and I wanted you to know. I am *not* going to break my habit of chewing gum. I am going to break my habit of chewing *Wrigley's* gum.

"I recently tried my first package of Sticklets gum and I enjoyed it very much. This experience happened to coincide with my receiving a copy of **SHOPPING FOR A BETTER WORLD**. When I saw how the Wrigley company compared with Warner-Lambert on so many important social issues, I knew that I had to make a permanent decision to change my brand of chewing gum. NO MORE WRIGLEY PRODUCTS FOR ME!

"As a lifelong resident of the Chicago area, I was not that surprised by the information about your company, but the booklet made it clear that your company is going to have to change its policies. Until it does I feel I must break the Wrigley habit and advise my family and friends to do the same."

(Letter to Warner-Lambert Co.)

"I recently received a copy of **SHOPPING FOR A BETTER WORLD**. I was both amazed and delighted to find how well your company was rated. And after comparing that to the very poor rating given to the Wrigley Co., I knew I had made a permanent decision. No more Wrigley's for me, it's Sticklets from now on. And I intend to pass the word along to family and friends.

"But first I wanted you to know. I am certainly not the only consumer who believes that we can "shop for a better world". I plan to do just that. And I feel that it is also necessary to thank you for your concern for your fellow man."

(Please send CEP copies of the letters you write.)

Letters to the Editors

How often have you wondered "What can one individual do?" Well, now that you know how each of us can make a difference every time we go to the supermarket, help spread the word! Let your friends and neighbors know about **SHOPPING FOR A BETTER WORLD** by writing a Letter-to-the-Editor (LTE) in your local paper. Tell them how you've changed your buying decisions, and how it has empowered you.

In addition to writing about corporate social responsibility, you can also use CEP's research to address such public issues as economic adjustment to military cutbacks, political action committees and the handling of toxic waste. Most small and medium-sized newspapers seldom discuss these issues. When you write a Letter-to-the-Editor you directly help stimulate and widen the debate on these vitally important matters. You'll assist us and your community by bringing CEP's informative research to many more people and making your own opinions known.

You can serve as a model to others. Encourage them to share information, to become involved, to spark a broader debate on issues that concern us all. For more information on how to become an LTE volunteer, please send in the coupon at the back of the guide. As an LTE volunteer you will receive free CEP Research Reports to help you back up your letters with facts.

Investing With A Conscience

As an investor, whether you have $100 or $100,000 to invest, you can put your principal where your principles are. Currently almost $500 billion are being invested using social criteria like those in **SHOPPING FOR A BETTER WORLD.** CEP's new book, *Investing In America's Corporate Conscience*, will help you integrate your values and your investment decisions. *Investing In America's Corporate Conscience* explains what "ethical investing" is, profiles its major exponents and innovators, and examines why it surged in the past decade and is still gaining momentum. It will discuss the motivating forces behind the social investment movement, and analyze the major "ethical" mutual funds.

Investing will compare the performance of 50 of the largest publicly-held companies and 50 companies most favored by ethical funds and investment advisors. This book will be a valuable resource for individuals like you, for investment professionals who manage socially screened accounts, and for institutions seeking to invest according to ethical criteria.

Look at your portfolio — do your investments reflect your values? What about the investment or purchasing policies of your church or synagogue, university or pension fund? For information about socially responsible investing and the release of CEP's newest book, see the order form at the back of **SHOPPING FOR A BETTER WORLD**

COMPANY ABBREVIATIONS

*Index to Company Abbreviations arranged
by abbreviation*

CLX . . . . The Clorox Company
CPB . . . . Campbell Soup
CPC . . . . CPC International
CRCH . . . . Church & Dwight
CS . . . . Celestial Seasonings
DF . . . . Dean Foods Company
DFAM . . . . Dolefam #
DIG . . . . Di Giorgio Corporation
DOM . . . . Dominick's Finer Foods
DOW . . . . Dow Chemical Company
DVF . . . . Deer Valley Farm #
EDEN . . . . Eden Foods #
EK . . . . Eastman Kodak Company
FAB . . . . Faberge, Inc.
FALC . . . . Falcon Trading #
FB . . . . First Brands
FFI . . . . Fantastic Foods, Inc. #
FL . . . . Food Lion
FLO . . . . Flowers Industries, Inc.
G . . . . The Greyhound Corporation
GAP . . . . . . Great Atlantic & Pacific Tea Company (A&P)
GE . . . . General Electric
GEAT . . . . Garden of Eatin' #
GEB . . . . Gerber Products
GES . . . . Great Eastern Sun #
GF . . . . Giant Food Inc.
GIA . . . . Giant Eagle
GIS . . . . General Mills
GMP . . . . Grand Metropolitan PLC
GP . . . . Georgia-Pacific Corporation
GS . . . . The Gillette Company
GTE . . . . GTE Corporation
GUC . . . . Grand Union Company
HEBG . . . . H.E. Butt Grocery
HERB . . . . Nature's Herbs #
HFF . . . . Holly Farms Corporation
HNZ . . . . H.J. Heinz Company
HOME . . . . Homestyle Foods #
HRL . . . . Hormel, George A.

HSY	Hershey Food Corporation
HVAL	Health Valley Natural Foods #
IBC	Iroquois Brands
IF	Imagine Foods #
JNJ	Johnson & Johnson
JPC	Johnson Products Co., Inc.
JR	James River Corporation
JSAN	John B. Sanfilippo & Son
K	Kellogg Company
KFS	Kanoa: A Free Spirit #
KLAB	Klaire Labs. #
KMB	Kimberly-Clark
KO	Coca-Cola Company
KR	The Kroger Co.
LFTI	Lifetone International #
LOMA	Loma Linda Foods
LOR	Loriva Supreme Foods #
MARS	Mars
MAYA	Mayacamas Fine Foods #
MCRK	McCormick & Company, Inc.
MEA	Mead Corporation
MEYR	Fred Meyer, Inc.
MILS	Miles Inc.
MMM	Minnesota Mining and Manufacturing Company (3M)
MO	Philip Morris Companies Inc.
MOB	Mobil Corporation
MOD	Modern Products #
MOUN	Mountain Ocean #
MUR	Murdock International #
NEST	Nestle S.A.
NEWO	Newman's Own. Inc. #
NFS	Natura Foods #
NOXL	Noxell Corporation
OAT	The Quaker Oats Company
ORJ	Orjene Natural Cosmetics #
OSC	Ocean Spray Cranberries, Inc.
P	Phillips Petroleum Company
PEP	PepsiCo, Inc.
PFE	Pfizer Inc.
PG	The Procter and Gamble Company
PP	Paul Penders #

```
PRD . . . . . . . . . . . . . . . . . . . . . . . . . . . . . . . . . . . . . Polaroid
PUB . . . . . . . . . . . . . . . . . . . . . . Publix Super Markets
QTX . . . . . . . . . . . . . . . . . . . . . . . . . . . . . . . Texaco Inc.
RAL . . . . . . . . . . . . . . . Ralston Purina Company
REV . . . . . . . . . . . . . . . . . . . . . . . . Reviva Labs. #
REVL . . . . . . . . . . . . . . . Revlon Group Incorporated
RG . . . . . . . . . . . . . . . . . . . . . Ralph's Grocery Company
RJR . . . . . . . . . . . . . . . . . . . . . . . . RJR Nabisco
RLM . . . . . . . . . . . . . . . . Reynolds Metals Company
ROR . . . . . . . . . . . . . . . . . . . . . . . . . . . . . . . . . Rorer
RP . . . . . . . . . . . . . . . . . . . . . . . . . . . Rachel Perry #
SAFE . . . . . . . . . . . . . . . . . . . . . . . . . . Safeway Stores
SANJ . . . . . . . . . . . . . . . . . . . . . San-J International #
SC . . . . . . . . . . . . . . . . . . . . . . Shell Oil Company, USA
SCJ . . . . . . . . . . . . . . . . . . . . . S.C. Johnson & Son, Inc.
SGH . . . . . . . . . . . Supermarkets General Holdings Corp.
SGP . . . . . . . . . . . . . . . . . . Schering-Plough Corporation
SJM . . . . . . . . . . . . . . . . . . . . . J.M. Smucker Company
SLE . . . . . . . . . . . . . . . . . . . . . . Sara Lee Corporation
SLGR . . . . . . . . . . . . . . . . . . . . . . . . . . . Solgar Co. #
SMC . . . . . . . . . . . . . . . Smith's Food & Drug Centers, Inc.
SPP . . . . . . . . . . . . . . . . . . . . . . . . Scott Paper Company
SQB . . . . . . . . . . . . . . . . . . . . . . . . Squibb Corporation
STOP . . . . . . . . . . . . . . . . . . . . . . . . . . . . Stop & Shop
SUN . . . . . . . . . . . . . . . . . . . . . . . . . . . . . . . . . . . . Sun
TBC . . . . . . . . . . . . . . . . . . . . . . Tasty Baking Company
TFC . . . . . . . . . . . . . . . . . . . . . . . . 21st Century Foods #
TILA . . . . . . . . . . . . . . . . . . . . . . . . . Tillamook Cheese
TOM . . . . . . . . . . . . . . . . . . . . . . . . . . . Tom's of Maine #
TOPP . . . . . . . . . . . . . . Topps Chewing Gum, Inc.
TWIN . . . . . . . . . . . . . . . . . . . . . . Twin Laboratories #
TYSN . . . . . . . . . . . . . . . . . . . . . . . Tyson Foods, Inc.
UB . . . . . . . . . . . . . . . . . . . . . . . . . . . . . United Brands
UBH . . . . . . . . . . . . . . United Biscuits (Holdings) PLC
UFC . . . . . . . . . . . . . . . . Universal Foods Corporation
ULAB . . . . . . . . . . . . . . . . . . . . . . . . . Universal Labs. #
UN . . . . . . . . . . . . . . . . . . . . . . . . . . . . . . . . Unilever N.V.
UPJ . . . . . . . . . . . . . . . . . . . . . . . . . . Upjohn Company
VH . . . . . . . . . . . . . . . . . . . . . . . . . . Vegetarian Health #
```

Giant Food Inc. .... GF
The Gillette Company .... GS
Grand Metropolitan PLC .... GMP
Grand Union Company .... GUC
Great Atlantic & Pacific Tea Company .... GAP
Great Eastern Sun # .... GES
The Greyhound Corporation .... G
GTE Corporation .... GTE
H.E. Butt Grocery .... HEBG
Health Valley Natural Foods # .... HVAL
H.J. Heinz Company .... HNZ
Hershey Food Corporation .... HSY
Holly Farms Corporation .... HFF
Homestyle Foods # .... HOME
Hormel, George A. .... HRL
Imagine Foods # .... IF
Iroquois Brands .... IBC
James River Corporation .... JR
Johnson & Johnson .... JNJ
Johnson Products Co., Inc .... JPC
S.C. Johnson & Son, Inc. .... SCJ
Kanoa: A Free Spirit # .... KFS
Kellogg Company .... K
Kimberly-Clark .... KMB
Klaire Labs. # .... KLAB
The Kroger Co. .... KR
Lifetone International # .... LFTI
Loma Linda Foods .... LOMA
Loriva Supreme Foods # .... LOR
Mars .... MARS
Mayacamas Fine Foods # .... MAYA
McCormick & Company, Inc. .... MCRK
Mead Corporation .... MEA
Miles Inc. .... MILS
Minnesota Mining &
Manufacturing Company(3M) .... MMM
Mobil Corporation .... MOB
Modern Products # .... MOD
Mountain Ocean # .... MOUN
Murdock International # .... MUR
Natura Foods # .... NFS

PRODUCT CATEGORY INDEX

Product .... Refer to chart headed:

A

B

Baby Oil & Baby Lotion . . . . see Skin Care Aids
Baco-bits . . . . see Salt, Seasoning, Spices
Bacon . . . . see Refrigerated Meats
Bagels . . . . see Bread & Toast
Bags . . . . see Paper Products
Baked Goods, frozen . . . . see Frozen Baked Goods
Bandages . . . . see First Aid
Barbecue Sauce . . . . see Condiments & Sauces
Bath Soaps . . . . see Soaps & Detergents
Batteries . . . . see Household Supplies
Beans . . . . see Prepared Foods
Beef, canned . . . . see Meat, Canned
Beer . . . . see Alcoholic Beverages
Beverages & Beverage Mixes . . . . see Soft Drinks
. . . . & Beverage Mixes
Biscuits, refrigerated . . . . see Frozen Baked Goods
Blades, razor . . . . see Shaving Needs
Bleach . . . . see Laundry Supplies
Body Lotion . . . . see Skin Care Aids
Bottled Water . . . . see Soft Drinks & Beverage Mixes
Bread Crumbs & Bread Products . . . . see Crackers
. . . . & Bread Products
Breakfast Cereal . . . . see Cereal
Breakfast Foods, frozen . . . . see Frozen Baked Goods
Breakfast Sausages . . . . see Refrigerated Meats
Breath Fresheners . . . . see Candy & Gum
Bubble Bath . . . . see Soaps & Detergents
Bubble Gum . . . . see Candy & Gum
Bug Spray . . . . see Household Supplies
Bulbs, Light & Flash . . . . see Household Supplies
Butter . . . . see Margarine & Butter

C

Cake, frozen . . . . see Frozen Baked Goods
Cake, packaged . . . . see Snacks
Cake Mixes . . . . see Baking Mixes
Canned Chili . . . . see Prepared Foods
Canned Fish . . . . see Fish, Canned
Canned Fruit . . . . see Fruit, Canned
Canned Meat & Chicken . . . . see Meat, Canned
Canned Milk . . . . see Milk, Canned & Evaporated

D

E

F

Light Bulbs . . . . see Household Supplies
Lighters . . . . see Household Supplies
Lip Care Products . . . . see Skin Care Aids
Liquor . . . . see Alcoholic Beverages
Lotion, Hand & Body . . . . see Skin Care Aids
Lotions, Shaving . . . . see Shaving Needs

M

Make-up . . . . see Skin Care Aids
Maple Syrup . . . . see Syrups & Molasses
Marmalade . . . . see Jams, Jellies, Spreads
Marshmallows . . . . see Desserts
Mayonnaise . . . . see Salad Dressings, Mayonnaise
Meat, frozen . . . . see Frozen Meat & Fish
Meat, refrigerated . . . . see Refrigerated Meats
Meat Sauce . . . . see Condiments & Sauces
Meat Tenderizers . . . . see Salt, Seasoning, Spices
Medicine . . . . see Proprietary Remedies
Metal Polish . . . . see Household Cleaning Compounds
. . . . & Sponges
Mexican Food . . . . see Prepared Foods
Mineral Water . . . . see Soft Drinks & Beverage Mixes
Mints . . . . see Candy & Gum
Mixes, Baking . . . . see Baking Mixes
Mixes, Cocktail & Beverage . . . . see Soft Drinks
. . . . & Beverage Mixes
Mixes, Stuffing . . . . see Crackers & Bread Products
Molasses . . . . see Syrups & Molasses
Mousse, Hair . . . . see Hair Care Needs
Mouthwash . . . . see Oral Hygiene
Mustard . . . . see Condiments & Sauces

N

Napkins . . . . see Paper Products
Nasal Spray . . . . see Proprietary Remedies
Noodles . . . . see Pasta & Rice
Nuts, Baking . . . . see Baking Needs
Nuts, Snack . . . . see Snacks

O

Oatmeal . . . . see Cereal
Oil, Cooking . . . . see Shortenings, Oil
Oil, Suntan & Baby . . . . see Skin Care Aids
Olives . . . . see Condiments & Sauces

Oriental Food . . . . see Prepared Foods

Puddings, frozen & refrigerated . . . . see Refrigerated
. . . . & Frozen Desserts
Purified Water . . . . see Soft Drinks & Beverage Mixes

R

Razors & Razor Blades . . . . see Shaving Needs
Relishes . . . . see Condiments & Sauces
Remedies, Cold . . . . see Proprietary Remedies
Repellent, Insect . . . . see Household Supplies
Rice . . . . see Pasta & Rice
Rice Dishes, frozen . . . see Frozen Vegetables & Potatoes
Rinses, Hair . . . . see Hair Care Needs
Roach Killer . . . . see Household Supplies
Rolls, refrigerated . . . . see Frozen Baked Goods
Room Deodorizer . . . . see Household Supplies

S

Sacks, paper & plastic . . . . see Paper Products
Salmon, canned . . . . see Fish, Canned
Sandwich Spreads . . . . . see Salad Dressings, Mayonnaise
Sanitary Napkins . . . . see Paper Products
Sardines, canned . . . . see Fish, Canned
Sauce, Tomato . . . . see Vegetables, Canned
Sauces . . . . see Condiments & Sauces
Sausages . . . . see Refrigerated Meats
Scouring Pads & Cleansers . . . . . see Household Cleaning
. . . . Compounds & Sponges
Seasoning . . . . see Salt, Seasoning, Spices
Shampoo . . . . see Hair Care Needs
Shoe Polish . . . . see Household Supplies
Sleeping Aids . . . . see Proprietary Remedies
Soda . . . . see Soft Drinks & Beverage Mixes
Softeners, Fabric . . . . see Laundry Supplies
Spices . . . . see Salt, Seasoning, Spices
Spirits . . . . see Alcoholic Beverages
Sponges . . . . see Household Cleaning Compounds
. . . . & Sponges
Spray, Nasal . . . . see Proprietary Remedies
Spreads . . . . see Condiments & Sauces
Spreads, Meat, canned . . . . see Meat, Canned
Spreads, Sandwich . . . . . see Salad Dressings, Mayonnaise
Stain Removers . . . . see Laundry Supplies
Starch . . . . see Laundry Supplies

EARTH DAY 1990 GREEN PLEDGE

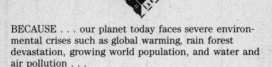

BECAUSE . . . our planet today faces severe environmental crises such as global warming, rain forest devastation, growing world population, and water and air pollution . . .

BECAUSE . . . the planet's future depends on the commitment of every nation, as well as every individual . . .

I PLEDGE TO DO MY SHARE IN SAVING THE PLANET BY LETTING MY CONCERN FOR THE ENVIRONMENT SHAPE HOW I;

ACT: I pledge to do my utmost to recycle, conserve energy, save water, use efficient transportation, and try to adopt a lifestyle as if every day were Earth Day.

PURCHASE: I pledge to buy and use only those products least harmful to the environment. Moreover, I will only do business with corporations that promote global environmental responsibility.

VOTE: I pledge to vote and support those candidates who demonstrate an abiding concern for the environment.

SUPPORT: I pledge to support the passage of local, state and federal laws and international treaties that protect the environment.

Earth Day 1990 — April 22, 1990

(To make your pledge please turn page.)

LET EARTH DAY KNOW THAT YOU HAVE JOINED
THOUSANDS OF OTHERS IN TAKING THE GREEN PLEDGE!

Signature

Name (please print)

Street

City   State   Zip

I also would like to support Earth Day 1990's campaign with my contribution of:

☐ $10   ☐ $25   ☐ $50   ☐ $100   ☐ Other _____

Please return to: Earth Day 1990, P.O. Box AA, Stanford, CA 94309

SBW

SURVEY

Now that you have had a chance to review **SHOPPING FOR A BETTER WORLD,** we would like to know how you feel about it . . . whether you've used it, found it helpful, have any ideas, thoughts and/or suggestions for changes we could make in future editions.

Please take a moment to answer these questions. Then cut along the dotted line and send this page to the Council on Economic Priorities, 30 Irving Place, New York, NY 10003. Changes were made in this edition as a result of our readers' suggestions. We want to continue to improve the Guide and we need your help.

1. What companies, products or brands not listed in **SHOPPING FOR A BETTER WORLD** would you like to see listed in future editions?

_____

_____

_____

2. Which would you prefer: (CHECK ONE)

   Brands listed within their product categories
   (the way they are in this book)?   ☐

   All brands listed alphabetically?   ☐

3. Which one of the 11 social categories on which CEP rated the companies do you think is the most important?

_____

4. What other social categories, if any, would you like to see companies rated on in the next edition of **Shopping For a Better World**? (SPECIFY)

_____

_____

5. Has **Shopping For a Better World** changed any of your shopping decisions?

Yes ☐   No ☐

(IF YES, PLEASE GIVE A SPECIFIC EXAMPLE, e.g., PRODUCT — ISSUE AREA)

_____

6. How often do the ratings in **Shopping For a Better World** influence your shopping decisions?

All the time ☐   Regularly ☐   Seldom ☐   Never ☐

7. What membership organizations do you belong to (e.g., Sierra Club, Greenpeace, etc.)

_____   _____

8. What other comments, if any, would you like to make about **Shopping For a Better World**?

_____

_____

_____

ORDER FORM

(all prices include shipping)

Additional Copies of "SHOPPING FOR A BETTER WORLD 1990"

Pocket size $5.95, or 5 for $18.00:   #_____ $_____

Full size: $5.95   #_____ $_____

Other Books by CEP

Rating America's Corporate Conscience $_____
  (Addison/Wesley; 1987; 499 pp; $16.95)

Pensions Funds and Ethical Investment $_____
  (St. Martin's Press; 1986; 163 pp; $17.00)

Star Wars: The Economic Fallout $_____
  (Ballinger; 1987; 350 pp; $21.95)

Hazardous Waste Management $_____
  (Island Press; 1986; 316 pp; $36.95)

Less 20% discount for CEP members $_____

Total: $_____

☐ Please send me information about CEP and a free Research Report (Specific interest: _____)

☐ Please put me on a mailing list for *Investing in America's Corporate Conscience.*

☐ Please send me information about CEP's Letters-to-the-Editors Program.

Name _____ Phone ( ) _____

Address _____

City _____ State _____ Zip _____

Visa/MC _____ Exp _____

Please send this form with your payment to CEP, 30 Irving Pl., New York, NY 10003. Or order toll free by calling 1 (800) 822-6435.

SUGGESTION BOX

The following are products I use frequently that I would like you to include in the 1991 **SHOPPING FOR A BETTER WORLD:**

_____

_____

_____

I would also like you to rate the following types of products:

_____

_____

_____

Comments/Suggestions:

_____

_____

_____

Please mail to CEP, 30 Irving Place, New York, NY 10003.
Thank you.

ORDER FORM ON FLIP SIDE